CONSUMERS' CAPITALISM

Consumers' Capitalism

and the

Immutable Laws of Economics

by Al Lax

Edited by Edmund A. Opitz

Chas. Hallberg & Company
Publishers
CHICAGO, ILLINOIS 60654

Standard Book Number: 873-19-008-4

Library of Congress Catalog Card Number: 70-82634

Table of Contents

Foreword

Charles Hallberg
Publisher

We challenge Black Capitalism, White Capitalism, State Monopoly Capitalism, Communism, and Fascism. We challenge any and all of the political concepts which promise an economic utopia based upon State intervention in the market place.

Here are the immutable truths of the economic phenomenon. Truths so *revolutionary* that no government on earth has ever allowed consumers' capitalism to flourish without restriction.

The author, Al Lax, learned his economics the hard way. He studied the writings of the great thinkers and scholars and, in addition, he learned from actual experience what is meant by the Marginal Utility Theory of Value (an economic concept more revolutionary in scope than any

Al Lax
Author

idea Karl Marx or John Maynard Keynes ever proposed) by working every day with that "thing" most scholars are protected from: John Q. Public, *the consumer*. In one of his enterprises, a department store, Mr. Lax competes in the market place to fulfill the wants of his fellow citizens for everything from aprons to zippers. In another enterprise, a finance company, he is called upon to solve the everyday money problems that plague you and me.

If you are aware of the problems facing our 20th Century civilization, I guarantee that the revolutionary concepts presented in this book will prove to be stimulating and thought provoking both now and in days to come as you apply to current problems the principals of *Consumers' Capitalism*.

x.

Preface

Leonard E. Read

Foundation For
Economic Education

Few businessmen are theorists; they do not have time to study the workings of the market, nor are they much concerned with the general conditions in a society which encourages freedom in exchanges.

They are specialists, and an overspecialized society is a fragmented one which courts its own dissolution, as Ortega y Gasset has maintained. Ortega directs his fire at scientific researchers who are learned in a narrow specialty but ignorant of all else, including "how society and the heart of man are to be organized in order that there may continue to be investigators."* He might have concluded, with equal validity, "that there may continue to be businesses."

Mr. Lax is an entrepreneur; he operates successful

xi.

businesses in California. Nevertheless, he has found time to master economic theory which he sets forth lucidly in the present volume.

Now, not everyone who strives to improve his grasp of political economy will write a book on it but unless more persons than now work at the task of upgrading their understanding of freedom—from which effort books will surely emerge—the future of liberty is dim indeed. This effort, however, appears to be getting under way, and is being made by persons from varying walks of life.

The present volume on basic economics is one of the visible results and is significantly encouraging because it proceeds from the mind of a successful businessman.

---

*Revolt of the Masses p. 126

Introduction

Edmund A. Opitz
Editor

Along with its professionals, economics is especially indebted to the amateur. It is not difficult to see why this should be so. The overwhelming majority of people go through life without writing a novel, painting a picture, or performing a laboratory experiment; but no one can avoid engaging himself in economic activity, for it is essentially the administration of scarce resources.

Economic activity is not out on life's periphery where one may indulge or not, as he chooses; it is squarely in the middle of the human situation, stemming from man's capacity for choice. Every man perforce engages in economic activity as he allocates his own time and energy, chooses between alternative uses of his talents. Such a central human preoccupation inevitably stirs some minds

xiii.

xiv.   Editor's Introduction

to reflect deeply on economic action and its implications, and the science of economics has, in consequence, been vastly enriched by amateurs.

David Ricardo was a stockbroker, Frederic Bastiat a statesman, William Stanley Jevons a logician, Philip Wicksteed a minister, and the great Adam Smith himself was a Professor of Moral Philosophy. These men broke new ground in economic theory and are best known to posterity for their contributions in this field.

Shoddy theories are deplorable wherever they occur, but they may crop up in astronomy or literary criticism, say, without directly affecting many people. But bad economic theory hurts us where we live day by day; no one escapes the disastrous consequences of popular economic error. The exposition of sound economic theory, then, is an invaluable contribution to the good life.

Mr. Lax is a businessman and an amateur economist. He runs a department store and a finance company, and knows what it means to try to anticipate consumer demand and to work with employees. This knowledge he has supplemented by wide reading in economic theory, and he has written a book which succeeds in putting that theory into understandable and down-to-earth terms. It deserves wide reading.

If we were to classify this present volume we'd put it within the Austrian School, as distinguished from the Classical or Manchester Schools of economics. What is the distinction? Early economic reasoning bogged down in the area of value theory, as it is called. When people are given a choice, their actions demonstrate a preference for some things over others. Why do they value A more highly than B? An 'off the top of head' answer might be that people prefer those items which they regard as most useful to them. But if this is so, how shall we account for the fact that people value gold more than iron, even though iron is a more useful commodity to mankind than gold? Try again. Perhaps a thing is valued in terms of the amount of labor that has gone into its production? But when we are mulling over the decision to buy or not to buy, the uppermost consideration is the item's importance to us; the toil which has gone into an item's production is the other person's concern, not ours. An eccentric genius might labor for years on a perpetual motion machine, and then have to pay someone to cart it away; whereas an idler might pick up a gold nugget and exchange it for hundreds of dollars. Despite the absurdity of the labor theory of value, Karl Marx made it the cornerstone of his system.

It was around 1870 that Jevons, Walras and Menger arrived independently at the *marginal utility theory of value*—a doctrine which the common man had practiced long before economics discovered it, as Bohm-Bawerk dryly observed. People attach a higher value to gold than to iron because they compare marginal units of the two goods; they do not compare the total quantity of gold with the total quantity of iron. And the same is true of

all goods. "At any given moment," writes Philip Wicksteed, "under the circumstances that then exist, the marginal values of all manner of things are arranged *de facto*
upon a scale which registers how much of this would
actually be accepted as equivalent to so much of that by
the individual in question, and at the moment; or if this
and that group of alternatives should be presented to him
which of them he will choose."[1]

A marginal unit of bread, or shoes, or whatever, is the
loaf or the pair lowest on your scale of values; it is the
most expendable unit, and thus the one you would exchange first. Exchanges occur because people want different things and want them with varying intensities; in
the course of exchange prices come to be attached to goods
and services.

The market value of each person's contribution is
assessed impersonally by his peers, their judgement mani-
festing itself by the amounts of their own goods and
services they are willing to relinquish in order to obtain
his. Capitalistic production, in other words, is round-
about. Few persons produce for their own consumption;
most of us specialize in the production of things which we
value mainly as our means for obtaining the things we
really want and need. (Speaking now of material production, not of intellectual and moral goods.) As Wicksteed
puts it, "Each of us accomplishes his own purposes more
fully by the indirect process of devoting a portion of his
energies to the accomplishment of the other's purposes on

condition that he reciprocates, than we could have done by each pursuing his own ends directly."₂

This is the market, the great emancipator of human energies and talents. Human beings cannot live without exchanging, so the rudiments of the market are always present. But a market economy is a rare development in human affairs; it emerges and is substained only when a significant number of people understand and meet its requirements. Mr. Lax contributes to that understanding by explaining, with great clarity, the workings of the market.

So much, then, by way of introduction; the book speaks for itself.

---

[1]*Common Sense of Political Economy, p. 122*
[2]*Ibid., pp. 134-5*

Part I

WHAT ECONOMICS IS
ALL ABOUT

Chapter 1

INTRODUCTION

General Confusion

With all the sciences and technologies the modern world has heaped so abundantly upon us, no field of thought has been subject to so much confusion and mystery as economics. Everyone gets into the act. Everyone also says something different. Attention is devoted to the economic pronouncements of politicians, scientists, playwrights, "The Average Man", and so on, ad infinitum. Each speaks with the booming authority of the thoroughly righteous who regards his own opinion as being just as good as the next man's—or somewhat better.

The implication that economics is a matter of opinion seems at first glance to be well founded. We are constantly exposed to conflicting economic testimony. For example, every four years at election time the out-party devotes long speeches and presents a formidable array of figures to "prove" what a sad shape the economy of the country is in. The in-party, quoting an array of statistics no less impressive, can "prove conclusively" that the economy is prosperous. (Often they use the same figures.)

At the bargaining table the labor union economist presents data and arguments to prove that the union wage demands are just and should be met. The economist for management presents equally forceful arguments that these demands should not be met.

More illustrations might be added but every reader can supply his own. Since there is so much disagreement among the "experts" one well may wonder who is right, who is wrong, and does any of it make any sense anyway?

If we look a little closer at these typical examples we can discern something interesting going on. The economists may be starting with a definite position to defend and may be seeking ways to propagandize for it. They are not engaged in economic truth-seeking but in trying to win a particular point. This process can occur on several levels, some more devious and complicated than others, so that it is difficult to determine what the economists' real goal is.

Anyone who takes a position and then calls up the "facts" of economics to prove it, is suspect. This is true regardless of how noble the position or how lofty the motive. Rather, the process works the other way around.

If the facts are examined and understood, the correct position will reveal itself. Most of the great blunders in the study of economics were made, are made, and continue being made by starting with a preconceived notion; then seeking to justify it.

Here we glimpse the crucial differences between economics and the natural sciences. Confusion and error must occur if, knowingly or otherwise, the methodology of the natural science is applied to economic problem solving. In the natural sciences it is the end result which is known through observation. Men observe the regularity of the sunset, for example, and in seeking to explain why this occurs they work back inductively to establish the principles—hypotheses and then laws—which explain the sunset. The laws are then tested by returning to the physical facts for comparison.

Economics, by necessity, works from the other direction. It is concerned with human beings and because human beings act and are observable, the principles of their activity can be known axiomatically; the logical implications of these observations must then be drawn to their proper conclusions.

In the preceding illustrations, if the economists for labor or management are set upon proving that a raise should or should not be granted, they may have to stretch or bend reality here and there as they go along in an effort to reach their preordained conclusion. The granting or not granting of the raise is not a fact similar in nature to the sunset. Economics cannot start with the end view—the sunset—and work backward. To be meaningful it must start with human beings living and acting here and now, and proceed from that point.

Once the starting point of economics is understood and its deductive methodology is grasped, further understanding ceases to be confusing and becomes a matter of following one logical step with the next. There are still difficulties aplenty, but the mystery is shorn away and economics becomes a subject for everyone.

The Descriptive Process

Having reviewed some of the confusion regarding economics we must now begin to avoid making the same mistakes, and to do this we start by understanding what economics is and what it is not.

Economics is a descriptive process. That is all. It tells something about man in a certain mode of activity; it is the story of man in motion providing for himself.

To see why this kind of story is of such vital interest it is necessary to begin at the beginning; that is, with man and some of the particular and special characteristics that make him what he is.

Man must provide the material to sustain his own life and the choices open to him are innumerable. All other living things receive food and shelter which chance puts in their way or, like the bees and squirrels, take rudimentary measures (within a narrow range) to provide for themselves. Man is unique among organisms for no other living creature has such a wide range of possible choices.

Man does not live in a Garden of Eden or in a land where manna falls from the skies in answer to his wishes. The sustenance for his life is available, though not unlimited, and man must find and convert this material into a form which will satisfactorily support him. As he goes about doing this he is always on the horns of a dilemma. He can convert only so much material and since it is scarce (or limited), to convert "A" this moment means he cannot simultaneously convert "B". Even if the material is plentiful, the converting factor (his labor) is limited, as is his time. So he has to make a choice.

This fact is preliminary to economics; it is an absolute which we have to accept and cannot change. Good or bad, it is the way the world is. And this positive fact of nature is the deciding economic influence upon every man alive.

To say that man has to provide the sustenance for his own life is equally true at every level of social activity. For an Aborigine this means having to find fruit for breakfast, pick it and eat it; hunt game for lunch, kill it, and eat it, etc.

For a twentieth-century New Yorker the materials needed for life are of a higher order and the means of achieving them more complex, but the basic necessities and consequences thereof are as applicable to the Gothamite as to the Aborigine. For both, the making of one choice excludes all other choices—*at that moment*. Thus, if the Aborigine decides to have fish for lunch he will go fishing. This decision makes it impossible for him to go hunting at the same time thereby having meat for lunch. In the same manner, the New Yorker cannot be an advertising executive and a butcher at the same time.

As it happened, man discovered long ago that some men were better fitted for hunting than others and the more these men hunted, the more skillful they became. It made sense for such men to specialize in hunting while others turned their energies to different activities. Thus, specialization within a division of labor began, and this specialization has been expanded and refined into today's system of division and subdivision of labor.

It is necessary to mention the division of labor here in order to see that while it claims a great advantage in making possible an enormous increase in production, it still does not change the fundamental nature of the question. Man must sustain his life and his means of doing so are limited.

Even within the framework of a highly advanced and specialized economy such as our own we cannot produce unlimited food, cars, or television sets. Thus, basic questions are raised which must be answered:

1. Because what can be made is limited,
     what shall we produce?
2. The division of labor makes for greater production, but within this division of labor,
     Who shall produce what?
3. And the first two questions imply the third:
     How shall the production be divided?

Economics is the description of the process which men use to answer these questions. This is the meaning of pure economics and it is in this sense the term will be used in this book.

The foregoing questions are really but one question which has been broken down, for simplicity's sake, into three parts. We may talk about phases of this question in order to examine the individual facets more closely but it must always be kept in mind (as will later be shown) that in real life all the parts are interrelated in such a manner as to render them inseparable. Economics, then, is an interwoven process.

The Relativity of Theory

Pure economic theory, or economic science, must be distinguished from several related but distinct disciplines.

Economic theory is not accounting. Accounting is an offshoot of economic action—specifically, of economic calculation; it arises out of economics and has no meaning except that which it derives from a theory of economics. To calculate that a store buys bananas for 7¢ a piece and sells them for 10¢ is part of the accountant's job, which is to total outlay and income, thus determining the viability of a particular business. It is by this kind of economic calculation that men find it possible to make use of the theory of economics for guidance in their day to day business activity.

The gathering of statistics is not economics. Statistics of economic activity always refer to past occurrences and the study of these may be correctly labeled Economic History. But without economic theory the collecting of figures would be no more than a meaningless list of numbers. Pure economics is the framework within which the economic historian can make his statistics come alive and explain something.

Neither can economics forecast the future and this is often one of the chief complaints against it. One hundred economists hold a year-end meeting and seventy-five predict prosperity for the coming year only to have a major recession begin. On the basis of this kind of performance enacted each year and various times in between, the question is raised as to the efficacy of any study of economics.

Economics, however, is involved in dealing with human beings, with men in motion. A chemist can predict the outcome of a controlled laboratory experiment but no one should expect any man in real life to predict the future of human events with absolute certainty. Postulates about future posibilities can be made—often extremely accurate ones—but economists, like any other men, are neither omniscient nor gifted with a capacity for fortune telling.

Most important of all, economics does not set ends. It does not pass value judgements. It does not say we should have high wages or low wages; a chicken in every pot or two chickens in every pot; or that we should have inflation, deflation, prosperity, or depression. The task of choosing the goals properly falls to the realm of philosophy, and through its derivatives such as morality and politics, philosophical ideas affect economic action. If it is decided that a chicken in every pot is a worthwhile objective, the decision has been reached by making a specific value choice. Once the decision has been reached, then economic knowledge may be called upon to devise the means necessary to reach that particular goal.

This point is a crucial one for understanding the details which follow. So often has economics been used to justify philosophical ideas it has become, in some quarters, a pseudo-philosophy. Actually economics is neutral as to end or goals; it can only tell men how to implement their philosophical ideas on the production-consumption level.

Economics tells us, within the setting of our civilization, how men answer the three basic quetions: Who produces? What do they produce? And for whom?

Because these questions are direct, it does not follow that the answers are, necessarily, equally direct. This may have been the case in the past but our modern world is complex and interrelated. Gradually some men came to perceive that because of this interrelatedness the results of a particular economic event or group of events could have varying consequences; and indeed, that the long-range effect could be quite different from what appeared as an immediate effect. Economics emerged as a science when men began to explore systematically these secondary ramifications. Economics is a determined effort to understand *all* the ramifications of economic events, both short-range and long-term.

Assume for a moment that the particular economic activity in question is like a snowball pushed from the top of a hill. If we see only the snowball rolling away from our feet we will not be aware of what takes place midway or at the bottom of the hill. If we want to know all about snowballs rolling down hills we must know its character and influence along its entire path until it comes to rest.

We cannot expect economics to tell us whether to push the snowball or not. That is the job of philosophy. Why someone might want to push the snowball in the first place is the job of psychology. Economics will merely endeavor to tell us what will happen if it is pushed; i.e., whether policy "A" will accomplish objective "B". It could tell us, for example, whether a minimum wage law will increase general prosperity over the short and long term, or what the effect of a tariff on sugar might be.

Short-range effects are immediately perceivable and are seen to follow as a logical consequence of the original action. The long-term effects are often not recognized as being linked to the original action but when the problem is thought through the logical connection becomes apparent. Thus, in times of wide-spread unemployment it may be proposed that half the unemployed be put to work digging ditches, and the other half be given jobs filling in the ditches. Further, it is proposed that they be paid by government for doing this.

The immediate consequence is that now there is no one

out of work and prosperity is seemingly created by all the new paychecks. A great deal of supposedly sophisticated economic theory will then attempt to show that this prosperity will feed upon itself in an ever-widening circle.

Economic sophistry is not what is needed, but economic common sense and a willingness to ask what the long-range effect will be. When such reasoning is applied to our example it becomes patently clear that men filling and digging ditches do not add to the production stream; in fact, so far as production is concerned they are doing absolutely nothing since one group cancels out the other. It should be self-evident that men doing nothing will not generate prosperity. They do not even provide for themselves and must therefore become a burden upon those who do produce.

It is necessary to add one last caution to the uses of economic theory:

In answering problems about short and long term effects, every answer has an implicit attachment which reads, "all other things remaining equal". Economics is a study of human activity and frequently "other things" do not remain equal. The economist cannot drag people into a laboratory and compel everything to remain static while he manipulates only one variable in the classic manner of an experimental scientist. He must deal with man in motion.

Chapter II

TO UNDERSTAND THE STORY

Man, the Actor

It is the concept of man in action which gives meaning to economics. All other forms of matter when presented with any situation can only react in the certain way specified by their nature (insofar as can be determined). Man alone has the capacity of choosing what he will do. There are limits to his choice but in normal circumstances the possibilities open to him are many. The idea of human action implies existence of choice. If there are no choices available, the motion involved becomes one of reaction.

Man involved in choice and action means constant movement, activity, flux, change, growth and decay. These are ingredients of all human life. It becomes clear then, that when we speak of economics (or man's economic life) the subject really being discussed is how man organizes that aspect of his life which is concerned with providing the material for his sustenance and enjoyment. Because of this intimate tie between economic and human life the importance of understanding economics becomes apparent.

Man engaging in choice and action necessitates the implication that this behavior has some attainable purpose; otherwise there would be no reason for making choices. A choice is made and the action assumed most appropriate is initiated. Man seeks to achieve whatever purpose he has selected through an action or series of actions; simply stated, he uses means to attain ends.

When we speak of man, the actor, we are talking about man, the *individual* actor. Only individuals may choose; only individuals are engaged in constant movement, activity, flux, change, growth, and decay. There is no such thing as an acting society. Society does not eat hot dogs, enjoy the movies, grow crops, make cars, or wage wars.

Individual man, acting in an individual manner, does all of these things. He may organize one kind of group or another, calling it a society, a corporation, a nation, or a gang; but as far as economics is concerned it is only the individual members of a group who act—never the group itself.

When we speak of the French, the New Yorkers, suburban society, or the masses, all we are doing is using a shorthand method of referring to a number of individuals whose characteristics are such that it is possible to conveniently classify them as a composite.

In a system based on the division of labor, it is often advantageous for individuals to organize themselves into groups, for the performing of functions which can best be handled in this manner. Likewise, one man may authorize another to act in his behalf. But in no case is individual production, or individual consumption, done away with and replaced by group production or consumption. Grouping together simply makes possible a potential increase in individual satisfaction.

This has to be so, because economics can only make sense as it relates to the individaul. The "economy" of the United States for example, can never be more than the aggregate economic results of each individaul member. Only metaphorically could it be said, "Because of a food shortage, the United States will go hungry this winter". The United States cannot be hungry, but individual within its boundaries can be. Neither can the Steelworkers' Union be underpaid, although individual steel workers might be.

Economics revolves around individual consumption, and production is defined as any step which advances goods and services along the route to ultimate individual consumption. A trucker, accountant, janitor, or librarian can be as much a producer as can an iron miner. Production is made up of innumerable individual productive acts as material, labor, and ideas are transformed and transferred into something consumable. Automated machines exist, but work only if created, directed, repaired and supplied by man. All machines can do is *multiply* productive effort.

It is sometimes said about the advanced western nations that the problem of production has been solved; that the citizens of these countries no longer need be concerned about production but only about consumption. The rationale for this is that to these people it seems our factories, farms, and mines turn out an endless stream of products by themselves. When we grasp that only individual man acts and produces we can see that if individual man stopped producing, production would stop also. Hence, the problem of production is not solved nor can it ever be.

While it is true that our modern technology has made possible an enormous productive capacity, at this time the world is not run by thinking and acting robots, but by thinking and acting individuals. Until the time when such robots take over, economics is concerned with man, the individual actor.

The Stage Is Set

Man, the individual actor, projects his movements within a framework. Part of this framework is judged by man to be beyond his control: The sun sets every day, the specific gravity of water is one, and so on. Man must leave these things as they are and accept them.

Economics is concerned specifically with those elements in man's environment which he can manipulate—things man *can* change in order to realize his goals. Man must work with these elements in order to sustain his life, and they narrow man's possible choices because these means are scarce, relative to human demands. They are economic goods because, unlike sunshine and air, they are available only in limited quantities.

One of the basic, all-encompassing limitations is time. Human life occurs in time and a man's time is always scarce. It is not unlimited. Man must apply his scarce time to the limited amount of potential sustenance material available in order to survive.

Sought-after goals can be achieved only in the future, never instantaneously; and the future is unknown. Thus, the great mystery of economics arises: How is man best to expend his resources or means (including time) now, in the present, so as to obtain maximum satisfaction both now and in the uncertain future? It would be a problem even for Robinson Crusoe alone on his island, and for three billion people spread over the earth the question (and answer) assumes fascinating proportions.

Traditional economics has divided economic goods into two classifications. There are consumers' goods or goods of the first order, and producers' goods, also called goods of the higher order or factors of production.

Consumers' goods are the end of the production stream; when the means have been converted into this form they are ready for consumption and the satisfying of wants and are no longer a concern of economics.

Goods of the higher order are broken down into the original factors of production, land, labor, and the produced factor, capital. Land and labor can be easily recognized as original factors of production (or as elements convertible into economic goods). Capital is produced from land and labor and necessitates examination in order to understand it in this economic sense; so as not to confuse *capital* with *money*.

Man learned long ago that certain things such as tools greatly increased his productive capacity. More and better tools made for more and better production. Thus, he sought to accumulate tools because although the making of them might temporarily curtail his current consumption—for he could not make tools and bread at the same time—in the long run the increase in output more than made up for temporarily curtailed consumption. By using tools man could expedite his engagement in round-about methods of production, producing chiefly for exchange rather than for direct use and thus further incease his output.

As the round-about methods of production have become more complex, capital has come to mean a good deal more than just tools. It can be a building (to house the tools), research, a trained worker, or fertilizer applied to land to increase the harvest. In short, capital can be termed everything which is used to keep round-about production going.

In accounting procedures it is customary to refer to

cash in the bank or cash on hand as "capital". Money itself is not capital in the economic sense—it is a medium
of exchange; and while it can be used to buy capital goods
in the marketplace, money is not inherently productive.
Gold, paper, or bank balances by themselves can produce
nothing. A nation short of factories and machines and
trained workers cannot create these factors of production
by printing additional money.

Throughout history one thing has made it possible
for man to evolve from a cave dweller, fighting with his
neighbor over a static supply of meat, to his present advanced state:

There has been an increase in production.

This increase has come about through an increase in the
amount of capital; without the accumulation of capital
goods man would soon return to the economic status of
a savage.

To those now living, the present standard of economic
life comes from capital previously accumulated—it is
partially a free gift from past generations. Some areas
have accumulated more capital than others. In the United
States the machinery is available to greatly extend individual output, which is why the American worker offering his services on the labor market can expect a much
greater remuneration than can his Chinese counterpart.
In China, production is low for the individual worker
because this capital is not available. Those who hold the
mistaken idea that labor makes wealth need only look at

countries like China and India where workers toil long hours at back-breaking physical labor, yet barely stay above starvation level. Production creates wealth; and accumulation of capital is the means with which production is increased.

What is Worthwhile?

As the history of economic thought developed, no problem was more pressing nor as difficult to solve as the question, "What is value?" No economic theory could be comprehensive without defining this most basic term. Various ideas were put forward, such as value in exchange, value in use, value arising from the labor put into an item, or value arising from the cost of producing an item. Each of these definitions was deficient in one way or another so that it was necessary to direct the search away from objective factors outside man and turn inward to his wants and demands—his own evaluation of his desires.

The answer, once stated, proved simple enough. Value arises because people want the item in question more than they want an alternative—when it is a case of having to choose one or the other. Value is an opinion stating the personal importance one or many persons attribute to an item. (Moral norms are sometimes referred to as "values", but this is another subject.)

Since, as we have seen, only man as an individual can perform economic acts, it follows that if he then proceeds to act on his opinions of what is worthwhile we will have a theory of value that is personal and subjective. An individual man always moves to satisfy whatever he feels to be his most pressing need at the moment. He alone knows what that is.

The individual actor is unable to have everything at once and, faced with choice, must decide upon the item he wants most before he can act. In formulating his wants he will necessarily rank his desires in a scale of preference: "I want Item A first, Item B second, Item C third", and so on.

The assignment of a rating to each potential choice is always on a first, second, third-choice basis; preferences are separate and dissimilar by nature and cannot be gauged by measurement other than a ranking order of importance, made by each individual, which is uniquely his own. First and second choices cannot be added to, subtracted from, multiplied or divided because this ranking of preferences is, in essence, the actor's decision that his first choice will give him the most satisfaction. Beyond that nothing more can be determined.

What is worthwhile is derived from the implication of human action. Since man always acts to fill that which he deems to be his most pressing need, by witnessing his action we can judge what his first choice was—under those circumstances and at that time. He may later find that he was wrong or that under different conditions he would have had a different scale of values, but during the moment of his action he has acted to obtain that which he desired the most.

This analysis of why a man acts to obtain the things he desires, in preference to something different, is completely individualistic and explains why, under what would seem to be identical circumstances, one man may do one thing and another something else. Jones may use Brand X toothpaste while his twin brother buys Brand Y time after time. Both are acting on their own scale of preferences. Persons living in a specific cultural environment might tend to acquire a similar orientation as to what is desirable but they act to acquire it only if they are themselves convinced it fulfills their most urgent need.

The subjective theory of value defies that kind of thinking which maintains a person should always do the "best" or "most appropriate" thing. Those who subscribe to this kind of thinking mean their own special brand of rightness. The next fellow is always doing for himself what he considers most reasonable. It may seem irresponsible or downright silly when viewed by someone else, but it never seems so to *him* at the moment.

Individual man's value scale may constantly change. It is clear that in the process of obtaining his first choice, new conditions are created that will change the scale of preference. Mrs. Jones wants potatoes for lunch; she goes to the market and buys some. From her action it can be determined that this is her most pressing want at the time. However, considering that she is thinking of lunch it is unlikely that she wants all the potatoes in the store. Certainly after obtaining some potatoes, more potatoes become less valuable to her. Upon buying, say, six potatoes, she has an ample supply; potatoes will no longer be her first choice and her desire will turn to something else.

At the point at which one additional potato would cause her to change her preference scale, that potato is marginal. In our example the seventh potato is at the edge, and is of marginal usefulness. Mrs. Jones would rather buy something else with her available funds than buy more potatoes.

All economic activity is orientated toward the satisfying of wants by consumption, which means that economic activity is pointed toward producing consumer goods. Consumer goods are valued by each individual according to his anticipation of the satisfaction he will receive by obtaining them. Then what of the value of goods of the higher order, those not used for direct consumption? They will be valued by the same individualistic process, except that the scale of preference will be based upon their estimated satisfaction or usefulness in producing consumers' goods.

Just how this works in detail—or stated another way, how economic value judgments control and direct man's economic activity—is the story to be told in the remainder of this study.

Chapter III

POSSIBLE CHOICES

Robinson Crusoe and His Island

To show how man goes about supplying his needs on a primary level, the example of Robinson Crusoe alone on an island is often used. In this example, every action Crusoe makes directly influences his well-being. It is a basic situation because the complications arising from the division of labor are not present to hide from view the results of Crusoe's activity. He is his own butcher, baker and candlestick maker, and if he does not make candles the nights will be dark. He cannot appeal to any agency that it is unfair for him to be without light and that he is therefore entitled to a subsidy for candles.

When first cast upon the island, Crusoe has going for him only his potential ability to perform labor, amplified

to some extent by his previously gained knowledge. He
has to apply himself to the general conditions he finds on
the island in order to survive. His first requirement will
be to obtain his minimum sustenance level and he must,
of necessity, do this immediately. Consequently he will
begin by producing goods which he can consume at once,
i.e., goods requiring the shortest period of production.

Crusoe finds there are coconut trees on the island and,
as he can live by eating these coconuts, he begins to gather
them. The coconuts are high in the trees and he must
laboriously climb the trees before he can discover and pick
the ripe ones. He soon determines that by spending ten
hours a day gathering coconuts he can harvest ten coconuts, or one per hour. He also finds that his minimum
sustenance level is eight coconuts per day but that ten
coconuts per day give him a nice, full feeling.

The rest of the day which could be devoted to work
(such as harvesting more coconuts) Crusoe devotes instead to leisure. In this sense, leisure is a consumable commodity and indeed an important one. Crusoe—or any
man—could conceivably work all the time, taking only
time out for necessary eating and sleeping. But men act
in such a manner as to indicate that leisure is a highly
desirable consumers' commodity. They will frequently
take leisure in lieu of more work and greater production.
It is purchased at the cost of less work-output. In a social
relationship one of the most sought after enjoyments of
a rising standard of living is less work time and more lei-

sure time. This can be accomplished in terms of fewer people working per family, shorter work weeks (or work days) or even a shorter working life, as expressed by taking a job late in one's youth and retiring earlier in one's old age.

Crusoe see vines and fallen branches on the island and believes he can make a ladder which will not only make coconut gathering easier but also make it possible to harvest more coconuts per hour. He decides to make the ladder and spends two hours per day at its construction. During the days he works on the ladder he gathers only eight coconuts per day instead of ten, since two hours are spent at ladder-making. Because he has two less coconuts to eat each day he has foregone consumption to this amount and invested his labor in capital accumulation (in this case, the making of a ladder). After forty hours the ladder is completed. The cost of the ladder was forty coconuts for this is what Crusoe could have produced with the forty hours he spent making it.

With the ladder Crusoe finds that he can gather three coconuts per hour. His productivity has tripled, and obviously he will not be long in making up the forty-coconut cost of the ladder since he can now produce, in a little over three hours, what previously took him ten hours. He may use this extra time for more leisure or he may turn his attention to other capital accumulation, to create other consumable goods.

During the forty hours Crusoe spent making the ladder

it should be noted he got no return at all. His capital accumulation was worthless until the ladder was in finished form and put to use as an instrument to increase productivity. His decision to make a ladder was based upon his expected return in the future. He preferred more coconuts in the future to less coconuts immediately. That was his time preference.

As Crusoe uses the ladder it gradually becomes a little weaker due to wear and tear. It depreciates. He may repair it as he goes along, investing more time at a cost of uncollected coconuts to keep his capital structure intact, or he may build a new ladder, again at the cost of uncollected coconuts, abandoning the old one at a certain point. In either case Crusoe will realize that his capital goods, the ladder, is used up in the process of producing coconuts. If he neither repairs the ladder nor provides for its replacement he then is consuming his capital a little each day as it wears out, and eventually will be back to gathering coconuts by climbing trees.

One of the problems facing Crusoe on the island is that the future is unknown. Should he invest forty coconuts (in foregone consumption) in a ladder, or would he be better advised to invest in, say, a net for fishing or a lean-to for shelter? He might discover a grove of oranges, or some coconuts growing closer to the ground in which case the cost of building the ladder would have been wasted; or a tropical storm might damage the coconuts in the trees so that they become inedible. If, instead of a ladder, he makes a net for fishing, he may be able to provide for himself with less labor and he might even like fish better than coconuts.

None of these alternatives can be known for certain and all Crusoe can do is assess the situation and act as appears to him best. If he misjudges and does the wrong thing his consumable goods will be less than they would have been otherwise and his standard of living will suffer. If he does the right thing he will be a success, with more consumable goods to enjoy.

Having sized up the situation, Crusoe will act upon the basis of his own value scale of preferences. The original alternative in our example was the immediate harvesting of ten coconuts per ten-hour day unaided, versus eight coconuts and work on a ladder (with the potential of a later increase in coconut production) per ten-hour day. He has shown by his action that the second choice was preferable to him at the time. Each period of time will present him with alternatives which he must rank on his scale of preferences and act upon. Should he build a net? Go swimming? Repair the ladder?

He will do whichever he expects will be most rewarding to him.

We have seen Crusoe start from scratch and, through savings (foregone coconut consumption), invest in capital accumulation (a ladder) and increase his production (more coconuts per hour). We have called this his time preference; his preferring more coconuts later to fewer

coconuts now. In this manner Crusoe enters into round-
about or capitalistic production. We have seen that capital accumulation, to be productive, must be used and in
being used wears out and takes continued new investment
to remain productive. Crusoe's decision to build a ladder
was an act of entrepreneurship, in that he had to forecast
future conditions and act thereupon.

We now look at Crusoe after he has been living on the
island for two years and find that he has been a successful
entrepreneur. By combining his labor with those resources
available on the island and restricting his consumption of
both material goods and leisure, he has become a capitalist.
His capital investment is in the form of a ladder for
coconut gathering, a net for fishing, a dam for the stream,
a boat for fishing, and a house.

In this situation, suppose Crusoe discovers some cleared
land suitable for farming and begins to farm. The ladder,
the boat and the net—a substantial part of his capital—
are no longer useful in providing his food since he will be
obtaining it by farming. What will now become of them?
The answer depends on the convertibility of the capital
item.

The net may prove to be useless for anything but fishing, and since fishing is no longer being done the net will
be abandoned. Crusoe may use the ladder as a bridge
across the stream even though it is not as good as a bridge
built for that purpose. He has the ladder and will put it
to this use, though he will not build another to replace

it when it wears out. The boat proves useful in exploring the island and if Crusoe did not already have a boat he would have built one. Capital accumulation accrued in the past and changed conditions may make this capital obsolete or partially so. Crusoe's decision to begin farming means that his capital accumulation must be viewed in a different light. If he abandons his net even though it is in good condition, he is not wasting his capital by alowing "unused" or "excess" capacity to exist; rather, he is devoting himself to something he considers better.

The Crusoe example is valuable for the lessons it demonstrates but in real life, of course, men do not live by themselves on islands. The benefits of specialization through the division of labor have been so overwhelming that the idea of a single man or even a small group of men living thus isolated has not been practiced. Still, the process of increased economic well-being, through increased production brough about by an accumulation of capital, is as valid for man in any societal organization as it was for Robinson Crusoe.

The Market System

Since man has rejected the idea of living completely alone, and instead resides within societies, we must now examine how man, in these societies, has solved the question of how to produce what for whom.

One of these ways is the market system, or a system of voluntary trading. A full voluntary market system has never existed but has been used in part. It is called the price system, free enterprise or laissez-faire capitalism. No one person invented the process; rather, it developed over the years. Its major shaping came during the industrial revolution and during the ninteenth century it reached its height.

The material achievements of man from the time of the industrial revolution to the present, practicing even a partial market system, has been astounding. From a state of stagnation and nearly universal poverty, so low and degrading as to be almost incomprehensible today, man in a few generations has raised his standards of living to the present lofty heights. Modern man lives better than the kings of old.

The outpouring of abundance continued while the population doubled, redoubled, and doubled again. Indeed it was the flow of material sustenance that made the population gain possible, since previously there had never been enough food to go around. Periodic famines and epidemics kept the population down. The increase of production was so vast it allowed not only increase in population, but the lifting of slavery and stultifying drudgery from the back of mankind.

Those countries which did not adopt the market system were left out of the bounty it bestowed, or received a comparatively slight overflow from their more prosperous neighbors. Today, those areas we call "backward" nations, whether comprised of jungle dwellers in Africa or the starving millions of the Orient, are the countries where the market system never took hold.

The market system is based squarely upon the concept of private property, without which it cannot exist. The owner of property goes into the market place and offers his property in exchange for property belonging to someone else. Thus, the idea of trade arises.

In actuality, the trader may resort to a medium of exchange, such as money, to facilitate his convenience in trading. In this case, one party to the trade is still swapping something he owns (commodities or services) for something the other owns (money) and the result is the same.

The concept of trade is applicable only to voluntary exchanges. If violence is used or threatened, then the exchange is not being entered into voluntarily and can no longer be considered a trade. A trade can occur only when neither party is forced to make the deal, when there is no coercion involved, and when either party may or may not swap as he chooses. Under these circumstances, a trade will take place only when *both* sides feel they profit from the exchange.

Mr. Jones has a loaf of bread which he offers to sell for $1.00 and Mr. Smith buys the bread, giving Jones $1.00 and taking the bread. In pricing his bread at $1.00, Jones has decided that in his estimation—at this time and in this place—he would rather have $1.00 than the bread. Conversely, Smith has, by his own judgement, concluded he would prefer a loaf of bread at this moment, to his

$1.00. A loaf of bread is higher on his scale of preferences than the $1.00. They meet in the market, make the exchange, and each regards himself as better off.

In the economic world, such exchanges are enacted constantly on every level and in every sphere of activity, and are interrelated with one another. Because they are all freely and voluntarily contracted we begin to see that the consumer is the man with the real power in this process. He is the one for whom individuals producing these goods must produce. He must be enticed with something he wants more than something he already has before he will freely and voluntarily enter into a trade to obtain it. In this manner, the market system answers the question concerning what will be produced—*precisely those items which the consumers most desire!*

In fulfilling those wants, the question of who will produce the goods is also answered. A consumer, in seeking to attain his wants, will patronize the producers whom he judges best able to satisfy them. From this process, a natural selection takes place among producers so that those who are successful in satisfying the consumers prosper; those who are not capable, fail. The market process comes full circle when answering the third question of dividing production, for only those producers best able to satisfy the consumers will find their products most in demand. Their efforts will give them more return than those of the less successful; with the greater return they are in a position to demand and obtain more of whatever the market has to offer.

This is true whether talking about the baking of bread, the making of an automobile, or the mining of lead. No less is it true if the product is labor—be it the writing of a book on economics or the digging of a ditch. If enough consumers feel that a particular book on economics answers their wants, they will buy the book, making the writer wealthier for his efforts. If enough people judge that the author's book does not satisfy their needs, he will soon stop writing and will turn to some other method of making a living.

The power of the consumer to influence economic decisions does not mean the consumer has unlimited power. If he is hesitant to buy a product offered on the market, competition among producers will act to reduce the price until he does buy; if the price is so low the producer cannot recoup his costs he simply does not produce any more, and the item is forgotten by both consumers and producers.

In the market system, certain men have found it especially advantageous to use capital as a means for increasing production. In effect, this will result in better goods at lower prices. The turning out of better goods at lower prices makes these producers great favorites of the consumers, enhances their individual prosperity, and thereby allows them to increase their own consumption.

We began by calling this process the market system. Because, in such a system, the consumer plays the domi-

nant role and because the formation of capital is one of
its major characteristics, a more descriptive term for it is
Consumers' Capitalism. Throughout the remainder of this
study, any reference to the market system will be so
designated.

The ramifications of *Consumers' Capitalism*, and how
it works, will be discussed in greater detail in Part II.

Socialism

There is another system man uses to answer the basic
economic questions. In recent years it has been called
variously, *Socialism, Communism, Nazism, Planned Economy, Dictatorship, Corporate State,* and other names.
These terms are all difficult to define because they are ordinarily used in a variety of ways, and to use them is to
become involved in philosophy, politics, and metaphysics.
These fields are all outside the scope of economics. Economics is not concerned with setting the ends men wish
to obtain, but only with the means they use to seek those
special ends which have been determined worthwhile.

Socialism and its derivatives is not new in human
thought. The ideas on which it is based go back to antiquity. But in the modern world, philosophical ideas are
expressed in economic activity and, in this manner, have
meaning for men as they live their daily lives. Thus, the
philosophies of *Socialism* and its offshoots have their particular way of being expressed in economic action and it
is this process that can properly fall within the examination of economics.

An analysis of the economic aspects of *Socialism* and its derivatives, show that they vary among themselves only in some relatively minor details regarding organization at one point or another. Actually, all these systems answer the basic economic questions in the same manner and it is this similarity which allows them to be grouped together for study. The method of answering the economic questions in these systems is direct and simple:

The Rulers, or Bureaucrats, decide who will produce what for whom.

The details may differ from place to place, with regard to how Bureaucrats may be chosen (i.e., through elections, force, or heredity); individual titles may differ, and the hierarchical structure may vary as to how much power the chief Bureaucrat may wield. Nevertheless, the process itself always remains the same—the Bureaucrats make the economic decisions.

Within the economic sphere, the individual acts in that manner which he deems best suited to fill his most pressing need. The rulers want the individual to act in a manner which will fit their own particular purposes; therefore in all systems of *Socialism* the leaders are constantly exhorting the citizenry toward cooperation.

Speeches and slogans can never do the job, for the differences between individuals seeking freedom, and Bureaucrats imposing control, are absolutely irreconcilable. If the system is to function, and voluntary cooperation is unattainable, then the rulers must resort to

ever-increasing force and coercion to make the controls
stick.

For this reason, a *Socialist* economy does away with, or
drastically curtails, the right of private property. If those
men who did not agree with the planners had the right to
own and dispose of economic goods as they saw fit, it
would be impossible for the Bureaucrats to plan the
economy of the nation. Voluntary exchanges and free
trade must therefore be eliminated.

In some forms of *Socialism*, the planners have had to
overcome the political disposition of the populace to
favor the right of private property. This has been done
by a semantic subterfuge. The individuals right to use
or dispose of economic goods has been limited, while continuing to refer to them as "private property". To the
extent that the right to use and dispose of economic goods
is limited, property rights are proportionately curtailed.

Whatever the advanced state of the planners, they have
been unable to increase production by writing reports or
making plans. No one is exempt from the fact that output per person can be increased to any great extent only
by increasing the amount of capital invested per person.
Through their controls, Bureaucrats are in a position to
accomplish this by making rules to govern which part of
the current production will be devoted to consumption,
and which part to producing goods for the accumulation
of capital.

The systems of *Socialism* with all of its variations, must

cope with the problem of capital accumulation no less than the system of Consumers' Capitalism. Because of this fact, and because, in this process, the Bureaucrats answer the three, key economic questions, we shall henceforth refer to these systems as *"Bureaucratic Capitalism"* and shall examine its workings in Part III.

Part II

CONSUMERS' CAPITALISM

Chapter 4

THE MARKET

The Invisible Hand

No one stayed up last night planning how the residents of the city of New York could have cream in their coffee today. No team of experts were bending over their figures deciding that X number of cups of coffee would be consumed and that ½X would ask for cream; that this meant such and such a number of quarts of cream must be available; and that the coffee shops, truck drivers, farms, refrigeration plants, container-makers and so on ad infinitum, must be alerted to the fact.

Rather, today the New Yorker went routinely about his business, drinking coffee at his pleasure, and always had cream when he wanted it. So it is with other things, be they shoes or ships or sealing wax. Somehow, there is enough.

Adam Smith, the first modern economist, has called this, the "Invisible Hand". It is the process by which men are allowed the widest possible choice of economic activity and yet coincidentally serve best the interest of their fellow man. How it happens is an amazing story. It is the story of *Consumers Capitalism* and the story begins, ends, and takes place entirely within the market.

To understand the market, we begin by examining what necessitates its existence.

That men differ in their abilities; that economic resources are spread around the world; and that men become better at their tasks by increased familiarity with them, are features of the general conditions of human life. In seeking the best utilization of these conditions men engage in specialization within a division of labor. Such specializing results in increased output per unit of input.

Within this division of labor, men perform certain functions. Later, we will discuss investors, workers, entrepreneurs, consumers, etc.—individuals in action within this division.

In the process of making a living, a man may frequently become several of these things. Obviously, everyone is a consumer and usually, everyone is also a producer. An individual who runs his own business is a worker, investor, entrepreneur, and consumer. When categories such as these are designated in economic analysis, it is for the purpose of referring to that man in the process of fulfilling a particular role, regardless of what other functions he might also perform.

One characteristic of the division of labor is that individuals do not produce directly for their own needs. The more economic activity becomes specialized, the more true this becomes. By specialization an iron miner may produce a mountain of iron ore; yet he cannot feed or clothe himself with iron ore. He must swap it for other items, and this creates a need for a swapping place: the market.

Swapping

Jones, the iron miner, comes to the market voluntarily, to swap his iron ore for different goods. Here he meets other men who have produced other things, and are seeking to do likewise. Under these conditions, exchanges are taking place.

Each individual has come with a personal list of preferences regarding the utility of the items he will be offered in trade. The utility of a commodity is its presumed value in terms of its ability to increase individual satisfaction. It has previously been shown that value is subjective, so for someone contemplating trade, the subjective use-value (what he thinks the item will do for him) is the prime consideration. He assorts the things he wants in a scale ranging from highest to lowest: from those which he desires most, to those he feels least inclined to obtain.

Suppose Jones has three 100-lb. sacks of iron ore to trade. He finds he can swap a sack for a cow, a sack for

a coat, a sack for potatoes, and a sack for a pair of shoes.
He must choose which course to follow. Let us say he
trades a sack of iron ore with Smith for a pair of shoes,
another sack for a cow, and elects to keep the third sack.
We can list the items on Jones' value scale as first, a pair
of shoes; second, a cow; and third, a sack of ore. Why
should he want to retain the sack of ore? Because from
his actions he has indicated that a sack of ore is preferable
to the item he would have gotten in exchange (in this
example, a coat or potatoes). Perhaps he plans to trade
his retained ore another day. Economics cannot say what
he has in mind; only that this is what he does, and that
these actions express his value scale.

Each man with whom Jones does business in the market
has his own private scale of values, just as Jones does. In
order to make the exchange at all, Jones must locate
someone who wants the commodity Jones has to trade,
more than he wants something he already has. Smith has
shoes to offer, and along his range of values he is willing
to trade a pair of shoes to Jones in return for a sack of
iron ore. In this example, the price of a sack of iron ore
will then be established as one pair of shoes. That is, a
sack of iron ore and a pair of shoes are equivalent for
exchange purposes.

Assume now, that on the market there appear more
men with sacks of iron ore to swap, and more men with
shoes to trade. How do they go about getting together?
How are prices established? The men with shoes to trade

will have their own evaluation as to what they believe their products are worth, as will the iron ore producers. Perhaps one shoemaker will be willing to give four pair of shoes for a sack of iron, another three pair, several others two pair, etc. We can visualize the aggregate of these individual value scales as being a schedule of demand for iron ore, ranging from the highest (in this case, four pair of shoes for one sack) to the lowest. Against this demand for ore will be that ore which is available for trade by the miners—the supply.

Traders in the market attempt to swap on the most advantageous terms. If the most willing buyer of iron ore (in our illustration, the man who will offer four pair of shoes for a sack) is experienced in the ways of trading, he will probably test the market by offering somewhat less than his best price in hopes of making a better deal. From the response, he can get a more accurate estimate of what he will have to pay for a sack of iron, since the iron miners have varying valuations for shoes and for the prices they will pay for shoes in terms of iron. If a previous exchange ratio between shoes and iron ore has been established which can serve as a starting point, the process will be simplified.

As exchanges are made between the shoemakers and iron miners, the price moves toward equilibrium. Realizing they need not bid so high to make a deal, the high bidders lower their price; while low bidders find no takers, so must raise their offers to make a trade.

Although trades may take place above and below the

final equilibrium price, the movement toward equilibrium is constant. As long as the demand for iron ore exceeds the ore being supplied for trade, the over-bidding of those seeking to obtain iron ore will push the price up. Conversely, if there is more ore available for trade than there are takers, the price will be bid down as the iron ore holders strive to unload it. The resulting equilibrium price is a balance where all who wish to sell can sell and all who wish to buy can buy. A technical term "The market is clear" describes this situation.

As a result of this process, the price (in the shoe/iron ore market of our example) is set. If there is now a change in the situation, making it more like real life where there is a constant, continuing change in market data, we have new supply and demand schedules to deal with and can expect the process to begin all over again— possibly coming to a different equilibrium price. If men begin to want fewer shoes, there is a fall-off in demand; and if the supply of shoes stays the same, the price drops as the market moves to a new balance.

The illustration used for economic goods has been that of a sack of iron ore and a pair of shoes. Men deal in goods in terms of serviceable units. There can be an active market for pairs of shoes, but except in rare cases of one-legged men there will never be a market for single ones. Thus, a pair is the smallest possible unit which has any meaning. Similarly, we have used as measurement a 100-lb sack of iron ore. Man might further break this down to fifty or twenty-five pound sizes but there is a point in dealing with iron ore at which the amounts become insignificant. Under normal circumstances men would not deal in grams of iron ore.

This explains why economics cannot reach the precision of a natural science, capable of being broken down into tiny atoms—units capable of being stated in mathematically exact terms. Economics can deal only in magnitudes large enough to influence man to act. Because these magnitudes vary for each item and circumstance, economics is perpetually describing a span of changing dimensions within which certain events occur—rather than reaching an exact and static point of minute differentiation.

Freedom in Trading

In seeking to get the greatest return per expenditure, it is the psychic return which men desire to maximize. This may or may not involve monetary return. Certainly there are many situations where a man will trade something the market considers valuable, for something of less or no economic value. If Jones were to give his retained sack of ore to his son, he would be receiving no economic value in return; however, psychic profit is not measured in this way.

Probably most human activity is directed toward areas beyond the economic realm to such things as love, beauty, friendship, and other intangibles which cannot be directly described in economic terms. Such actions pose no problems for economic analysis, however, if we remember that psychic return is what men strive for, and that it can sometimes be achieved through economic action. Because of its ability to buy time, as well as material goods, monetary return is used as a means to increase non-economic profit.

Jones can trade for economic goods to whatever extent he has something to trade in exchange; or more concisely, his income must match his outgo (not including gifts or loans). This simple fact is one of the cornerstones of *Consumers' Capitalism*, and simultaneously the basis for the most emotional attack against it. Yes, Jones is free to trade, the argument states, but he is also free to starve.

This statement taken by itself is true, but not in the way usually implied. For to be free in the market means an absence of physical force, coercion and fraud, and the right of Jones, or any individual, to conduct his affairs without being hindered by someone else. That one is free to starve is a condition of nature and exists regardless of whether there is a maket or not.

The market is a device to help alleviate this condition, by allowing Jones access to the fruits of other men's specialization, just as they are allowed access to his. Because the market exists, it does not follow that the market must somehow make available to Jones anything and everything he wants, any more than it means Jones must make available on the market anything and everything someone else wants. The market does not create or guarantee plenty; it is only an exchange post.

Furthermore, it is voluntary. If Jones believes the market is treating him shabbily, he can retire to an isolated state (as was outlined for Robinson Crusoe) where he does not enter into trade with his neighbors. He is apt to discover, in so doing, that his standard of living will be reduced to existence at the "coconut and fish level", since he no longer has the benefits of other men's talents nor even the full potential benefit of his own.

Similarly, to be free in the market does not mean that Jones can decide he wishes to be like General Motors, somehow arranging to have all the equipment, know-how, and material provided for him in order that he might match this large enterprise.

Rather, it means that Jones will be unhindered in building a kindred company if he wants to; doing so through his own efforts or with the voluntary cooperation of others.

If he decides upon the latter course of action, freedom in the market does not mean he will then be automatically successful in swapping the automobiles he produces. All traders in the market are unhindered, and will individually decide whether or not to trade with Jones for his automobiles; their decisions will indicate where competing automobiles rank on their own scales of value.

The market is neutral. By itself it changes none of the general conditions of human life, nor does it change human valuations. By itself it does not produce abundance.

It is a method of operation—a tool—which men have devised to expedite their economic activity; it has no life of it own, and, outside of this function, has no meaning whatsoever.

Purchasing Power

The action of Jones and Smith in going to the market to trade has several manifestations. Each will be better off if he has more to trade. Jones has concentrated on mining iron and Smith on shoe-making, precisely because this is the way each can produce more, have more to trade, and thereby improve his standard of living. Each produces, in order to consume.

The never-ending, day-in, day-out battle is to wrest from nature as much abundance as possible, in order to consume as much as possible. To suggest that man should consume in order to produce is economic nonsense.

Smith, realizing he can obtain more goods if he has more to swap, will strive to enlarge his production. This will increase his purchasing power. But suppose everyone in all lines of endeavor increases production, so that total output is generally greater. Will there now be too much? Will the market be "flooded" with goods to the extent that not all of them can be absorbed, because there are not enough buyers with purchasing power? Of course not. For as each individual increases his production, he increases not only the supply available, but simultaneously, his own buying power.

In this way, production creates its own demand. In our

example of the iron ore/shoe market, let us assume that this year each miner and each cobbler has doubled his output. The over-production bogey would lead us to believe that catastrophe will result. Such is not the case, for when they meet to swap, the price-setting mechanism will work as before—only now, each will come away from the trade with twice as much in real goods.

Herein is the basis for the fact that in a free market system, every increase in production benefits everyone, which is another way of saying that the more there is to consume, the greater consumption will be. A person may lose sight of an output gain if it is scattered over a sizable economic area; often it can best be seen in retrospect.

Any increase in supply (other things being equal) means prices are lower than they would have been otherwise, and no matter how limited an individual's purchasing power may be, it is thereby strengthened. Conversely, every falling off in output makes everyone poorer. Every fire, every strike, costs each member of the economy something, though it may be so little as to go virtually unnoticed. A major flood, famine, or war not only can wipe out those directly affected, but will reduce the standard of living of entire populations.

Chapter 5

WHERE PRICES COME FROM

Money is a Convenience Commodity

We have traced the beginnings of the market to individual value estimates expressed in direct swaps. These
barter transactions are the first steps in an exchange economy and, in primitive parts of the world, are still used
extensively. Before going further in our examination of
the developed maket, we must introduce the concept of
money; because the use of money makes possible the evolution of an economy beyond the barter stage.

The term "money" in everyday English, has several
meanings. It can mean cash in our pockets, our bank
balance, our net worth, funds invested in the stock market, etc. In this discussion, money has a definite, specific
meaning:

Money means a medium of exchange.

Money, *as a medium of exchange, is neither capital nor wealth;* if we keep this in mind we can untangle the mystery associated with this commodity.

As men engaged in barter, sooner or later it became apparent that certain commodities were sought after more than others. In one society, salt was such an item and men perceived that it was advantageous on occasion to trade for salt, with the expectation that at a later time the salt could be exchanged for other commodities. In such a manner, mediums of exchange were developed. Whether the commodity used was shells, furs, wampum, or other valuables, it always performed the function of making trading easier.

Gradually, certain commodities came to be recognized as better fitted to serve as a medium of exchange than others. Ideally, such a commodity should be somewhat more scarce than most items, requiring time and effort to find and/or convert from nature. It should be relatively imperishable, easily handled, and capable of being divided or added to. Universal acceptability ideally fits a commodity to become a medium of exchange. As civilization advanced, people more readily accepted certain luxury goods—notably, gold and silver——and these emerged as the best mediums of exchange.

There always were and still are secondary mediums of exchange, such as diamonds, but gradually gold has moved to the position of eminent acceptability. People value gold for its own sake (as jewelry and for ornamentation), above and beyond its metallic use in industry. And they value it because it can be universally exchanged for the other things they want. Thus, gold has become money.

We have excellent testimony as to how well gold has fulfilled its historic function of serving as a medium of exchange, and how widespread is is acceptability. Throughout the world, gold is eagerly sought and held by governments and individuals alike, and in the case of the latter it is often held even when illegal to do so.

However, gold as a medium of exchange has disadvantages; it is inconvenient to carry around in large amounts and its ready acceptability and homogenous quality makes it necessary to protect it from thieves. So gold warehouses, or banks, came into being. Here, men could deposit their gold for safe-keeping, thereby receiving a warehouse receipt for the gold on deposit. These gold certificates were considered claims on the gold actually deposited, and were circulated as money.

The development of money is one of man's most ingenious inventions. Because of the existence of a medium of exchange, a man with an elephant who wants a locomotive does not have to wait until he finds just that certain individual who has a locomotive and wants an elephant. He swaps his elephant for money and, with money in hand, can more easily locate and do business with a locomotive seller. The medium of exchange permits a man to swap a commodity of limited marketability (such as an elephant) for one of more universal usage, such as money.

Two corollary effects emerge when money is being used as the medium of exchange. First, money becomes a standard of value; that is, the money commodity is used to gauge the value of all other economic goods. It is only through the process of money evaluation on the market that exchange ratios of various goods can be known. If wheat sells on the market for $1.00 a bushel and cotton for 50¢ a pound, the exchange ratio of one bushel of wheat equaling two pounds of cotton is thereby stated in monetary terms.

Secondly, money also becomes a storehouse of value. Since it is the trading commodity par excellence it can be traded for and held with the expectation of being easily swapped for other economic goods at a later time. Current production by the individual can thus be exchanged for a medium which will be useful in the future to meet anticipated or unanticipated needs.

Demand and Supply

For convenience in trading, and for a means to compare one item to another, man has devised money. It enormously simplifies matters to be able to perform economic calculations in money terms, stating the exchange ratios in dollars and cents. However, to say that wheat is selling for $1.00 per bushel is not enough. We must understand why it is selling for $1.00, rather than 10¢ or $10.00 per bushel.

Prices are the connecting links, the joiners, which intertwine all market processes. To see how prices are formed we can proceed with our example of Jones, the miner, and Smith, the shoemaker.

With the introduction of money, Jones and Smith now enter the market to make indirect exchange. They will swap their respective ore and shoes for money; then, with the money, buy those things they want. Each still has an individual value scale (now expressed in terms of money) with the aggregate of these value scales making up the demand schedule for any given economic good.

Demand schedules are likely to be elastic; i.e., the lower the price, the higher the demand—and the higher the price, the lower the demand. This happens on an individual level because for each consumer the lowering of a price means he need give up less (in terms of foregoing other goods) to obtain the item. Thus, the item will more probably fall, within the scope of his value scale, at a place where he will take action. If shoes are selling at $5.00 a pair, Jones may buy one pair and then decide that his $5.00 bills can better be spent on other goods. But if shoes are selling at $3.00 a pair, he may buy one pair of shoes; then decide that for $3.00 he would rather have another pair than some other item. Or it may be that at the $5.00 price, Jones does not wish to buy shoes while at $3.00 he may decide a pair to be worthwhile.

The essential element is, that as prices go lower people are tempted to buy more, whereas when prices rise they buy less. The demand for each commodity may be more or less elastic, depending upon the nature of the item itself.

Interacting with the demand schedule of the buyer is the supply available for sale. The buyers compete, as in an auction; those most interested in the commodity will be willing to pay the highest price for it. If there is only one unit on the market, the purchase will be made by the highest bidder. (It is in this manner the price is arrived at for a Rembrandt painting.)

Ordinarily, many units of supply are available for sale as men constantly engage in selling and buying, consuming and producing. The supply can be elastic for the same reasons demand is elastic. When Smith gets $3.00 for each pair of his shoes he may not be interested in making the effort to produce more. But if the price goes to $5.00, he might regard as worthwhile an extra effot to increase his output of shoes and, based on a $5.00 selling price, he would be in a better position to secure more shoe-making men and materials. The market seeks to balance supply against demand, demand against supply, in so doing, the prices move toward equilibrium—that point at which all who want to buy can do so, and all who want to sell can find buyers.

Since the price of an item is that point at which demand equates supply, there can be no such thing as a "fair" or "equitable" price. What one man fancies to be a "fair" price, the next man may not. But the market process is concerned with the whims of neither—it is concerned solely with finding that level where the sellers can all find buyers, and buyers can afford the sellers' wares.

As a result of changing conditions in the market, the demand and supply schedules are subject to constant fluctuations. Differing tastes, desires, style demands, and the varying wants and needs of the consumers act to change demand—either weaking or strengthening it. Stronger demand against the same supply will raise prices, as the increased demand results in more bidding; weakened demand will lower prices, as fewer seek the available goods.

New inventions or methods of production may increase the supply of a good, and if the demand remains the same the price will become lower. Whenever there is a change in data, the market process takes the new information into consideration and seeks to find a new level of equilibrium.

The market is hastened to a state of equilibrium not only by buyers (seeking to obtain items for immediate use) and sellers engaged in trade; but also by buyers and sellers who seek to profit by discovering where the market is not in equilibrium. Men engage in arbitrage (buying in one market and selling in another) whenever a discrepancy in prices between these markets offers an opportunity for profit. In so doing, they add to demand where the price is low and to supply where prices are higher, speeding the arrival of the equilibrium balance. Speculators, convinced that future prices will be higher, buy now with the intention of selling later. To the extent they anticipate correctly, their actions tend to smooth out fluctuations in the price, strengthening present demand and increasing the present price; later their actions may serve to add to supply when the price is higher, thereby lowering the price.

Sometimes it is fallaciously urged that the cost of production sets prices. One need only consult a department store buyer as he takes his mark-downs, a manufacturer with hula-hoops to sell, or someone with a warehouse full of 1920 calenders, to see the error in this approach. Once goods are produced they are "costless", in the sense that whatever factors of production were used in making them were expended in the past and are irretrievable in their original state. Present goods exist in the present; if someone is stuck with 1920 calendars, any selling price obtainable is better than nothing even if it proves less than the original cost of producing the calendars.

An increase in demand against the same supply exerts upward pressure on the price, but if this happens to an item with an elastic supply schedule, the higher price will act to cause more of the item to come on the market. If demand slackens against an elastic supply, the supply will tend to diminish due to lower prices. If there is very little demand (as in the case of 1920 calendars) the item will disappear from the market.

Producers will not continue to produce an item for which selling price is below costs of production plus a profit. Thus, the cost of production can influence the supply which may be made available through new production and may set a limit on such new production, but its influence is only an adjunct to the supply-demand relationship in setting prices.

It is true that costs may be considered by businessmen in figuring their selling prices. Such actions are one means through which a businessman may estimate the market. He assumes that competitors have similar costs and that he will therefore not be overpriced by setting his selling price from cost; or in calculating that he must recover costs plus profit to maintain the venture. What the businessman is doing, in these instances, is calculating an *asking price*. The customers, by their actions in buying or not buying, will tell him whether, like the department store buyer, he must take a mark-down.

It costs as much (or more) to make silk stockings as to make nylon hose but this has nothing to do with the price either will bring at the market-place. The consumers decide the price for each, and when they show by their actions that silk stockings will not bring prices sufficient to cover the cost of making them, the manufacturers quit turning out silk stockings; thereby releasing their labor and facilities to be used in making nylon hose or other items.

Within the supply-demand framework, production costs are an unerring, never-failing guide for determining what to produce, even though by themselves they do not set prices. Costs become regulators which guide the market into allocating the factors of production in the best possible manner. Produced economic goods are the result of a directed bringing-together of labor with the material factors of production, over a period of time. Costs of production are merely expenses involved in the process.

It should now be apparent that if the cost of production does not set prices, neither do wage costs, which are only one part of production costs. Proposals that money prices be eliminated in favor of some other form of calculation (such as labor units) do not fall within the market system. For in *Consumers' Capitalism,* prices are ultimately set by individual subjective value judgements: Mr. White asking, "Is is worth it to me?" before he buys. The item may be heavier or lighter, smaller or larger, take ten minutes or ten hours to make; yet Mr. White will still ask the same question.

The Role of Competition

The attitude toward success and failure, held by some, is such that they see in one man's advance another's decline. This attitude is carried over into economic life which is viewed as a "rat-race", a primeval jungle of vicious, clawing, cut-throat competition—where it is necessary to smash the opposition or be eaten. The true state of affairs in a system of *Consumers' Capitalism* is just the opposite. Competition is the force which protects all the people. It is the hidden benefactor permeating the market organization; the guardian, which keeps it in line with the wishes of consumers.

Men are not natural enemies. The magnificent overflow from present-day production, when compared with economic life a few centuries ago, is conclusive evidence of the advantages men can secure through working together. The striving of one individual against another in the economic sphere serves the interest of everyone. For onè who fails in economic competition, there awaits neither firing squad nor Siberia. He is simply assigned—by the consumers— to a more modest place in the economic system, and even this outcome need be only temporary.

In the market the consumer is the protagonist. He is the ultimate chooser, the one who, in effect, orders goods to be made. He is the one who must be satisfied; the one for whom the producer must produce. He is the final customer, who is always right. The production process is aimed at producing something the consumer will find acceptable.

The consumer exercises this power by picking from the goods available those which he considers best able to satisfy his needs. This sets in motion a chain of events which effects not only the retailer with whom the consumer deals directly, but the suppliers, wholesalers, manufacturers, etc., with whom the retailer deals; and, in turn, the many other sources along the line of production.

The individual consumer, in seeking to fill his most urgent needs, will buy the best available goods at the cheapest possible price. A supplier able to bring off this deal will be successful, but to attain such success he must be an efficient producer.

From the countless variety of raw materials available to him he must work up the product best suited to the particular requirement of his customer. By striving for efficiency in the manufacture of a product pleasing to consumers he exerts pressure on his suppliers of raw materials and capital goods.

If Smith is a shoemaker and wants to continue in that line of work, he must sell shoes which are at least comparable in sales appeal to what others are offering for sale. In seeking to put his shoes on the market he must pick, from the factors of production, those items (in the necessary amounts) which will enable him to accomplish production of marketable merchandise. He must choose the leathers, laces, labor, machinery and hundreds of materials necessary for making shoes that will be competitive. He does not buy the leather he personally might prefer for his own use; he buys the kind which will result in saleable shoes.

His action, then, in buying or not buying one or several types of leather; in choosing among various kinds of labor; together with many other such decisions; influences the suppliers. He is their customer. They, in turn, influence the suppliers from the next stage of production. It is thus that the consumers' desire to buy a competitively-priced pair of shoes is transmitted upward through the various production levels in such a way that these stages of production are made to conform with the wishes of the consumers.

The producers must always work to fill the needs of the consumers. Through the selection process the less able producers are weeded out, leaving only those best able to satisfy the consumers. If Smith cannot make shoes at least as efficiently as the next shoemaker, he will find few customers and will eventually fail. Hence, the producers constantly strive to arrange the factors of production in a more efficient manner to meet or beat competition; and this action moves the maket toward that perfect state wherein all factors of production will be used in just the proper ways.

This is a state, however, which the market can never attain. No sooner is one path taken than others appear. New inventions, processes, techniques and discoveries—as well as changing needs, tastes, wants, and desires—are continually surfacing, making a whole new mass of market data available; thus, causing a shift in the market.

One of the complaints against *Consumers' Capitalism* is that it is a hard, cruel and capricious system. If this were true, it would only be because people are that way. Actually, it is not true. In buying from those who offer him more for less, the consumer is simply stating his individual value preferences which, in the free society of *Consumers' Capitalism*, he has every right to do. It is not unreasonable for a consumer to prefer to buy from an old and well-known company if it sells something better for less; conversely, if a new company offers something better for less it is just as reasonable to expect the consumer to desert the old supplier in favor of the one offering more for the money. If the service is better, and the prices for the same merchandise are cheaper at the supermarket than at the corner grocery, we can expect the supermarket to have more customers.

When comparing the supermarket with the corner grocery, the consumer's right to choose is obvious. A law giving special advantages to the corner grocer would be recognized as unjust. Yet, when we begin to consider the price of labor, and the right of the consumer to direct economic choice towards those who offer better labor and service for less, there is likely to be a howl of protest. Nevertheless, the principle holds as true in the one case as in the other.

Another part of the cruelty charge leveled against *Consumers' Capitalism* is that in the process of change entire groups may be left behind. The candle industry was faced with virtual extinction when the light bulb was invented; with the innovation of the automobile blacksmiths were in for a rough time from the new competition. With the introduction of computers, thousands of businesses and jobs were threatened.

The only way to prevent this would be to forbid all progress—an idea which hardly needs comment. Historically, however, there has been a mitigating factor, in that the market is so wide and the wants of the consumers so varied there is usually a demand for seemingly bypassed items.

In addition, the new never takes the place of the old overnight. Thus, candlemakers had time to convert to

other occupations after the introduction of the light bulb
(and while consumers gradually changed over to electric-
ity). Even to this day candles are being made.

Competition works on all levels within the market.
There is competition among the sellers/producers to offer
the best for less to the buyers. In choosing from their offer-
ings, the consumers set up a process of natural selection
which favors the most efficient sellers/producers. When
the market is free, some men are always in position (or
waiting in the wings) to take over, if those presently
efficient become inefficient. Similarly, the consumers and
buyers do not have unlimited license; they must bid
against each other for the goods available in the market,
and in so doing they will establish a competitive price.

Hence, competition on all levels takes the whim out of
economic activity. Where there is competition, an individual buyer cannot name a price, however high or low,
and expect to buy so long as there are other buyers also
eager to obtain the item who will pay more. Likewise, an
individual seller cannot name a price, however high or low,
and expect to make a sale so long as there are other sellers
more willing to sell. Competition distills the fantasy from
economic activity, causing it to correspond to a reality of
aggregate human wants, set against collective human
possibilities.

Despite this, the market system is so broad any individual may disregard competition and the market to do as he
chooses; but to the extent that he does so he will be penal-

ized economically.

If we see White, the "Beer Baron", bustling around his brewery, hiring, buying, selling, saying "no", he appears to be the master of a feudal estate. A closer look shows the error of this concept. White is dependent upon people who buy his beer. If his customers stop buying his beer tomorrow, White will soon have no brewery. If he were to persist in a policy of attempting to sell beer at such a price that few could afford to buy it, the visions of a feudal barony would go up in smoke to be replaced by visions of bankruptcy court.

If he should choose to pay double wages to those working for him and finds he is losing money, his philanthropy can last only so long as there is money in his estate. If he should decide to fire all his competent help and substitute members of his notoriously lazy family, he can do so only at the expense of putting himself in a competitively disadvantageous situation, which will adversely affect his business.

Competition is keen in the labor market, and its existence explains why men, whose skills are needed by consumers, see the price of their work bid up. Competition is also the reason why no worker has to accept cruel or unfair treatment from an employer. He is free to leave what he considers an inequitable situation and offer his services on the competitive labor market, expecting to receive the going-wage for his type of labor service.

No less does competition affect the owners of capital.

If they wish to maintain their funds and enjoy the proceeds of its contribution to the productive process (in the form of interest and dividends), they must take care to invest with caution. If the ventures in which they invest do not supply what the consumers want, the ventures will not make profit; hence, will not be able to pay interest and dividends and even the original investment may be lost. The owners of capital become intermediaries for the funnelling of investments into undertakings which the consumers approve.

It is frequently said that competition is unfair because all men are not equally equipped to compete. This is an immutable fact; a general condition of nature. Not everyone is born with the ability to play big-league baseball, hit .400, and earn a six-figure salary. Neither is everyone born with the ability and drive necessary to achieve whatever degree of success he fancies is his due. Some men are born to—or may devlop—wealth, intelligence, pleasing personalities, ambition, good looks, common sense, or any of a long list of qualities which may or may not help one in financial competition.

These factors are all outside the scope of economics. The consumer is concerned with getting what he considers the best possible value, and is not usually concerned with how a particular supplier has achieved his degree of efficincy. Rarely would we expect to find a consumer saying, "White's beer is better than William's beer and costs less, but I buy William's beer because William is such a

lousy beer maker". Or, "White's beer is better than
William's, and costs less, but I buy William's beer because
William is a poor orphan who supports his mother-in-
law and fifteen children."

Time

Economic problem-solving for human beings occurs not
only in space (that is, broadly, on the surface of the earth)
but also in time. Time is a basic constituent of life, and
consequently is also a basic constituent of economic activity. As man engages in lengthened production processses
where labor and materials are moved through stages of
decreasing remoteness to the final consumable product,
time is involved. Capitalistic production takes longer.

Jones, the iron miner, is not only geographically distant
from the buyer of a steel knife which his iron ore helped
make, but also distant in time. Man values time; indeed,
perhaps as much—if not more—than anything else. We
shall now examine how man expresses this value of time in
economic life.

All other things being equal, there is, in the acting man,
a universal desire for economic goods to be had sooner,
rather than later. That this time preference exists can be
easily understood by contemplating the fact of consumption; if it were not preferable to consume now as opposed
to later, no consumption would ever take place! Rather
than consume today, it would be put off until tomorrow
and when tomorrow came with a new decision, it would
be postponed until the next day, and so on.

With eating and other necessities of life, it is, at the very least, impractical to put off consumption—as some minimum must be consumed to maintain life. With any excess above the level of mere subsistence one can exercise a choice as to whether to consume now or later, but still, all other things being equal, goods are preferable sooner, rather than later. It is better to have steaks today, rather than tomorrow; have a home in the suburbs this year, rather than next; and to join the county club now, rather than five years later.

In the modern economic world, goods are reduced to evaluation in money prices for trading purposes, which makes possible a further comparison of the value of present to future goods. Time preference means that $1.00 now is preferable to $1.00 a year from now; and it is even more desirable to have $1.00 today than to have it twenty years from now—all other things being equal.

All other things, however, are not equal. Time preference, working through the trading mechanism, sets up a state of affairs where today's $1.00 will be worth, say, $1.06 a year from now. This difference in the price of present and future dollars is called the discount of future goods against present goods. One would have to pay $1.06 a year from now to borrow $1.00 today. The price—i.e., the size or spread of the difference—is set (as are all other prices in *Consumers' Capitalism*) by demand and supply. The demand comes from those wanting present goods; whereas the supply is furnished by those who possess present goods but are willing to forego the present use of these goods, in order to get a greater future return.

This fundamental category of action gives rise to interest and ultimately sets the rate of interest. (In the preceding example, the interest rate was 6%.) It also make possible expansions of the production process over a length of time. If there were not some men who would prefer $1.06 next year to $1.00 this year, everyone would produce for immediate consumption only; and there would be no way to "carry" goods in partly finished but inconsumable stages of production from one time period to the next. Lengthened processes of production with their higher output per unit of input would not exist.

This process can best be illustrated by imagining a great cloud of radioactive material settling over the earth which would eradicate all life in a month's time. In such a situation, there would be no counter-balance to time preference for immediate goods, and no demand for future goods beyond thirty days, no matter how high the interest rate. All production of future goods would cease.

Chapter 6

THE PRODUCTION STORY

Land Earns Rent

In examining *Consumers' Capitalism* we have thus far discussed the necessity of exchange in a specialized economy and how, in general, supply and demand affect such exchanges. Now we shall look into the specific effects of supply and demand on the various factors of production to see how these are tied together into a process of creating what people want. This is the story of production.

One of the basic factors of production, and one of the areas from which production (and wealth) originates, is land. By land, we mean natural resources such as land, water, oil, ore, native metals, etc. Beyond that, when natural resources are mixed with labor and/or capital (which is frequently done in the production process), it is no longer solely land, in the economic sense. A fertilized, fenced, and irrigated farm represents not only the factor, land—but other factors which human labor has added to the land, in order to bring it several steps nearer to production of consumable goods.

Income accruing to land is called rent. By capitalizing the value of rent, the selling price of land is obtained. If land A rents for $60.00 per year and the going interest rate is 6%, it would have (all other things being equal) a sale price of $1000.00. A person investing $1000.00 in Land A would, in this way, receive a 6% return, or the current interest rate.

An individual will pay rent for land, or capitalize its rent and buy it, because he expects to use the land factor in producing goods and services. Speculative purchase and holding of idle land follows the same rule; in this case the holder is merely anticipating use at a later date. In either event, the limit to what will be paid for land is set by its anticipated contribution in creating the goods and services for which is employed. Those seeking to use land can afford to bid up the price to the point where use of the land will still show a profit, but not beyond.

In finding this level of marginal profitability in the use of land, the speculator is guided by the consumer, whose demand influences the price of the products which land is involved in creating. Higher prices for the goods and services which land helps to create means higher prices for the land. The prices of these products are thus reflected in the price of land. Since the consumer is the ultimate customer, his wish is passed up the chain of command by translation into product prices which eventually set the price of land.

There might be land which is not considered profitable for use at the present time. Two hundred years ago, on the American continent there was a great deal of land in this category. It was considered too remote; there was other land more easily accessible for satisfying the demand for natural resource products. As demand increased, this heretofore sub-marginal land became valuable, and was put to use.

Where land is convertible, it will be put to those uses which consumers esteem most highly. Land in the environs of Los Angeles is suitable for either orange-growing or homes. Visitors from snowy climates may be dismayed to see beautiful groves falling before the bulldozers; however the consumers' desires reign supreme in usage of this land for homes—as indicated by the developers' ability to over-bid the orange growers.

Several hundred miles away, in the middle of the Mojave Desert, there is cheap, unused land. The consumers do not presently regard the goods and services to be derived from this land as being worth very much, so the land is consequently of little value.

Land has certain special characteristics. There are some thing which cannot be produced without it—for example, homes in the suburbs. Land is not mobile, and this factor can decrease or increase the value of specific parcels, depending upon the demand in each case. For example, land in suburban Los Angeles is more valuable than land in the Mojave Desert. Its fixed position and fixed amount of area make for an inelastic supply. Higher prices for this land cannot increase the overall supply which has been determined by nature; consequently overall demand is the final, determining factor in the price of land.

Beneath this overall theoretical level, in the present situation land use is more elastic than would appear at first glance. Higher prices will cause more unused land to be placed on the market although it may be more remote— even to the extent of leveling mountains, draining marshes or dyking the ocean. Higher prices for land will also cause available land to be used more productively (in effect, increasing the supply) through intensive fertilization, construction of high-rise buildings, etc.

Another characteristic of land is seen in the case of depletable natural resources. Some products which come from the land such as oil and coal are irreplaceable in the nomal course of events; once used, they are destroyed in their natural form and gone forever. Does the present use of such assets mean we are stealing from future generations?

In actuality, this is a nonsensical question. For under the terms implied in such a question, this year's usage of either one barrel of oil or one million barrels would constitute stealing, and who is to say what pace would or would not be tantamount to stealing from future generations? No one is omniscient and can forecase with final accuracy what future needs will be, or what future developments will determine future needs.

The price for these depletable assets, as has just been shown, is set by demand and supply which, in *Consumers' Capitalism*, determines the rate of consumption of these resources. If some people foresee shortages they can, under a market system, purchase and hold such assets until the shortages do develop; the market process will then reward them for their foresight by making them rich.

The fact that people aren't willing to do very much of this type speculation signifies how uncertain the future actually is. It is no trick to multiply yearly oil consumption by known oil reserves, and arrive at year X when there will theoretically be no more oil on earth. But who would be willing to bet *his own money* that by year X more oil, or substitutes for oil, will not have been found?

These special characteristics of land are not enough to segregate it to some exalted station above economic analysis. Land is still only one of the factors of production; and, as such, is used to create economic goods in the same way other factors are used. The price of land is derived (as is the value of the other factors) from the evaluations placed on it by man in action.

Labor Earns Wages

Many erroneous theories have been put forward to explain how wage rates are set, including the following postulates:

a. Workers should receive enough to keep them alive.
b. A skilled worker should make X times the rate of an unskilled laborer.
c. Wages should give workers enough to buy back the things they produce.

By and large, these are not economic theories, but philosophical-social ideas, advocated for special purposes. They are based upon, and receive emotional response from, the misunderstanding that in *Consumers' Capitalism* the workers are treated, at the employer's whim, as chattels, non-entities, and wage slaves; and are paid from a fixed fund.

A worker is an individual human being; not a commodity. Under a free system, he is the owner of himself and, as his own owner, also the owner of any labor he performs. In a specialized economy characterized by exchange, he may choose to swap his labor for some other economic good and this labor service which he swaps on the market is a commodity, just as the service of land or capital is a commodity.

The economic category of labor includes all work done in the process of creating and moving economic goods toward a consumable state. For purposes of economic analysis, the services of a corporation president, psychoanalyst, or ditch digger are all labor, and this labor commodity has a price on the market—just as do all commodities. And, like other commodities, the price of the labor commodity is determined by supply and demand.

We have seen that a producer producing for the market is dependent upon the customers who buy his product. He must remain competitive to stay in business, and cannot raise his price by whim. He must also make a profit. Consequently, when he purchases those factors for use in making his product he must pay careful attention to cost, weighing the cost relationship against his final selling price.

In this manner, an unhindered employer will seek to use the factor of production (labor service) by hiring additional workers for his enterprise, until he reaches that point at which costs are so great he cannot get a refund from his customers. When he cannot make a profit on the labor service provided by the last worker hired, he has passed the point of 'worker marginal productivity', and will hire no more. Until that point is reached he will continue to hire additional workers because his profit is inceased by doing so.

When wages are higher than they would be if set by the demand-supply relationship, the marginal productivity of labor drops. The employer soon reaches the point where he cannot hire more workers, because their cost of employment, plus his profit, will not be returned to him through the selling prices paid by his customers. As a result, there will be people looking for jobs for whom no work is available. When these job seekers find no employment they reduce the asking price for their services, and wages go lower until it finally becomes profitable for employers to hire them. Thus, everyone who wants to work can obtain it, and the price of labor is in balance.

Conversely, if wages are too low employers will seek to increase profits by hiring additional wokers. This action will bid up the price of labor until it is in balance with the existing supply-demand relationship.

There are variations in the quality of service performed by individual workers which arise from differing aptitudes, training, skill, experience, etc.; these differences are given weight by the market because the consumers consider some services more valuable than others, and are willing to pay more for them. A surgeon receives more for his labor than a ditch digger, not because of the long training period which surgery requires (as is often believed), but because people consider this service more valuable. The long training period in this case acts to influence the supply of surgeons, consequently influencing the demand-supply relationship.

Actions within the market place indicate that consumers have placed a relatively high value on the services of certain workers. Some public figues, such as movie stars, opera singers, baseball players and others high in public esteem, receive high wages for their work. Whether they arrive at this lofty status by virtue of birth, self-discipline, or sheer luck is not a subject for economic commentary. The factor pertinent to economics is that such people must maintain themselves by selling their services, and would soon fall from favor (thereby being

forced to accept lower wages) if the consumers became
unwilling to pay for these highly specialized services.

Under certain conditions, labor can be the most mobile
factor of production. It can shift from one kind of service
to another. A rock-and-roll singer can become a ditch
digger, or vice-versa, often with comparatively little
retraining. Since demands of the consumers are constantly
changing, the mobility of labor becomes an important
consideration.

As changes in demand and supply occur throughout the
economy, one effect is an increased demand for labor
service of a certain kind in one area; a decrease in demand
in another area; etc. This fluctuation personifies variations
in the wage rates between different kinds of jobs; with
those skills most in demand and in smallest supply com-
manding the higher wages. The difference in wages
persuades workers to leave the lower paying fields, in favor
of gaining employment in higher paying endeavors. In
this manner additional workers are encouraged to enter
those areas which the consumers have shown they prefer.

The greater the difference in wage rates, the more pronounced this tendency will be; and the less specialized
skill and training necessary, the sooner it will occur. Thus,
we would expect many ditch-diggers to shift to gardening
if a significant wage differential arose; in a field like
psychoanalysis, with a fifteen year training period, the
tendency would not express itself overnight. Over a given
length of time differential wage scales will tempt more of

those who are readying themselves to enter the labor market to prepare themselves for the higher-paying jobs. Coupled with normal retirement, this means that the labor force is gradually shifting to those pursuits most approved by consumers.

One of the implications inherent in each man's being a self-owner is that he may choose not to offer his labor service on the market. When production per person is low, this implication has little practical meaning for not working means starvation. But in an economy of high productivity, conditions arise that do permit the efficient individual to choose the combination of work and leisure he prefers. After earning enough to live on, a person may then decide to work less and enjoy more leisure, rather than working longer hours for additional money to spend. Leisure becomes, in this sense, a consumable good.

Judging by the experience of the western nations in the past two centuries, leisure has been a much sought-after consumable good. As production rose and more goods were provided for more people men began to enjoy an increase in leisure time. A standard was reached—sufficiently above the starvation level—so that it was no longer necessary for children to work in factories, and parents were able to support their children's leisure.

Later, still higher production allowed the husband to support the family on his work alone, so wives did not need to work. Finally the husband's working week and work day were shortened. All this happened because real income per hour of work increased, and men elected to enjoy some of this increase in the form of leisure.

The system of *Consumers' Capitalism* carries the most effective kind of unemployment insurance possible. We have seen how the force of the market is always toward equilibrium—that point at which all who want to work can find jobs and all who want to hire can find workers. A surplus of people who want to work but for whom there are no jobs, is completely foreign to a free system and could not occur.

This does not mean an individual would be guaranteed getting just that certain job in that particular industry, located in a specific town, at the exact wage he wants. Rather, it means that on the prevailing market there are always opportunities for jobs. What (or where) these opportunities may be, is determined by the consumers.

In reviewing job possibilities, workers may weigh subjective factors which do not show up in the dollars and cents price. These may include such considerations as the time and place the work is to be performed, the status assumed to be associated with the job, the comparative pleasure of the work, or any other special meaning the worker may attach to a job. For example, more people prefer a job paying the same wages, if employment will be in California rather than Alaska.

Consumers, through variations in wage rates, exert pressure on workers to perform the services which they (the consumers) most desire—at the time and place they want them performed. Although an individual worker is free to do whatever type of work he wishes, this freedom does not extend to being able to decide his employment with impunity. If he chooses an occupation which the consumers have judged less important he is penalized economically by receiving a comparatively lower money price for his services.

There is no such thing as "technological unemployment", when this term is used to denote a condition wherein men cannot find jobs because they have been replaced by machines. There may be temporary technological displacement, when machines accomplish part of the work which had formerly been done by men. The effect of such displacement is similar to a change in consumer tastes or desires. Fewer people are employed in one area, and are thereby freed to seek work in another.

The truth of this statement is illustrated dramatically by looking at one of mankind's greatest technological break-throughs and labor-saving inventions: the development and adaptation of the wheel. Where, in history, has been recorded unemployment—caused by the use of wagons for transport, instead of the backs of men? And where in present-day living is unemployment being caused through the use of cars and trains, rather than wagons? Indeed, this illustation indicates that if men wish to increase their economic well-being, the need is for more labor-saving inventions, not fewer.

There is a positive, dynamic force favoring those who

offer their labor service on the free market. Labor is the scarcest factor of production. There exist more natural resources and more productive processes—both real, and potential—than there are people to convert them into useful commodities. As science opens new fields of economic endeavor, and as capital accumulation multiplies the efficiency of human labor, this condition becomes even more pronounced. The marginal productivity of labor is raised, so that consequently employers can—and must—bid ever higher prices for labor. In the long run, net productive gains (more production per person) show up as increased wage rates and accrue chiefly to labor.

This fact make it possible for almost any person to obtain work in a developed economy which will return him a living wage. Enough capital has been invested to raise worker productivity above the subsistence level.

In the United States (which is considered the world's most highly developed country), there are idle farms, idle factories, unused resources. Because of the comparative labor shortage at present, some unused material factors of production could be expected. If, however, such a condition exists alongside people who are looking for work, but for whom there are no jobs, then *Consumers' Capitalism* is not the villain, but something else. Many people regard such a situation to be a cruel economic phenomenon, and we shall examine it further in Part IV.

Capital Earns Interest

Capital comes about from a combination of land and

labor. These factors of production are brought together primitively at first, as Crusoe did when he added his labor to vines to make a ladder. This process then becomes an additional factor of production, capital or tools; and may be further combined with land and/or labor, and/or capital in more complex forms, until it emerges as something very sophisticated—an automated factory, for example. The hoped-for result of the process is an increase in production (more unit output per unit of input), or the production of something which could not have been produced otherwise.

Clearly, the use of capital factors such as tractors and fertilizer increases the food output per unit of land and unit of labor employed, although food could be produced without their use. Equally clear, moon rockets could not be produced at all without an enormous amount of capital accumulation invested in their production. In brief, capital buys the time, tools, and transportation necessary to raise man's standard of living.

Capital comes from savings—that is, foregone consumption. Some people decide that rather than consume everything they produce right now, they will save it for later enjoyment. In examining the phenomenon of time preference, we have already discussed how future goods are discounted and how, through paying of interest, the choice the individual must make is whether to consume now; or wait, and have more goods to consume later. By way of the price mechanism, this choice is translated into money; those who forego consumption in an exchange economy do so by saving money.

This "saved" money, representing a surplus of current production over consumption, can be used to purchase capital. The capital purchased in this manner, in actuality will be the surplus of current production over consumption—the savings. In other words, the amount of current production in excess of consumption (responding to the demand from savings), has been created in a specialized form called capital.

Those who save may invest their savings directly by using it in their own businesses, by loaning it to another business, or investing it through intermediary marketing organizations organized for this purpose. These marketing organizations are banks, insurance companies, savings and loan associations, credit unions, etc., and in modern times they have become so efficient that any individual's saved dollars, however few, can be put to use. When these marketing companies (or individuals) have obtained the saved funds, they seek to put them out for utilization on the loan market.

On the basis of utilization, loans are classified as either consumer's loans or producer's loans. In consumer's loans, the money is used to buy consumer goods (cars, refrigerators, clothing, vacations, etc.). Jones saves some money and puts it in a savings account in the bank; the bank loans it to Smith, to finance Smith's vacation. In this instance, no capital accumulation has taken place from

Jones' savings, since Smith uses the money for his vacation (present goods). Smith was enabled to fly now and pay later by paying an interest charge; showing by his action that at the time, present goods were worth more to him than future goods. Jones receives interest on his savings account, getting more in the future for his present goods. The bank charges Smith more interest than it pays to Jones, which is its fee for making the arrangements.

The demand for production loans comes from businessmen, engaged in their roles of arranging the factors of production to best satisfy the consumers. They use the borrowed funds to obtain additional machinery, to increase their inventory, etc., and are guided in their decision as to whether or not to borrow the money by the profitability of their product. If investing additional capital will create more profit, the indication is that steps should be taken in that direction.

By supporting a price for the product which makes such investments profitable, the consumers have given their approval to disposition of additional capital in this manner. The businessman, for his part, expects to pay the cost of the loan (the interest charge) from the additional profits he will make through use of the loan. He will not pay more interest than he expects to make profit, so that his consideration is turned toward the marginal productivity of capital. He will seek to borrow up to the last dollar on which he can earn more than the interest charge will cost.

Once money is available on the loan market, the price of
a loan, or interest rate, is determined by the demand of
those seeking to use the funds, set against the available
supply of such funds. By demand, we mean the demand
from those individuals whom the lenders consider able to
repay the loan.

Since the possibility of non-payment is ever present, it
is customary, in economic analysis, to break down the
price of a loan into the pure-rate of interest (which is the
amount charged on a riskless loan) and the risk-factor
price (a kind of insurance against non-repayment). In
this way, borrowers who are regarded by the lenders as
less secure will pay premium prices, and these prices are
themselves determined by the demand and supply
relationship.

The marginal productivity of capital varies from company to company and from industry to industry. Those
firms whose profits are highest on invested capital are in
a position to bid higher in order to borrow additional
capital for use in their enterprises. Those businesses with
comparatively low returns cannot pay as much for loans.
In this way capital tends to flow into, and serves to expand, the higher profit businesses. These are the businesses
the consumers most approve, as their higher profits
indicate.

The additional capital will expand production of the
higher profit businesses, while less capital (usually in the
form of replacement capital) is going to the lower profit

businesses, lessening production there. Such actions bring prices down in the bigger profit areas as a result of increased competition through increased production; while the opposite is taking place in the low profit industries.

In this manner, the flow of capital tends to push toward a uniformity of profit rates in the economy as its flow influences the contraction and expansion of specific businesses and industries. Within an industry group, however, an especially efficient producer—because of his comparative low cost production—would still enjoy higher-than-average profits. Like all equilibrium rates in *Consumers' Capitalism*, uniformity of profits is never fully reached. New directions appearing in the economy, as a result of changing conditions, open up different or newly emphasized areas for higher profit possibilities, and the capital market reacts accordingly.

If the price of loans is too high—that is, if the interest rate is higher than it would be if set by the demand-supply relationships—the lenders will find they have idle funds on their hands. In attempting to unload their lendable merchandise, they will lower the price, in order to entice borrowers. As the price goes lower some who would not borrow at the higher rates come on the market seeking loans. (Since the interest rate is composed of both pure rate and risk-rate, lowering of the price might be done by leaving the interest percentage the same, but granting loans to those previously considered sub-standard risks.)

This process continues, until it reaches a balance where

anyone seeking a loan can get one and those with money to lend can loan it out. If the interest rate is lower than that which would be set by demand-supply relationship, the opposite effect occurs and the movement toward equilibrium is begun.

To be productive, capital must be put to use, and with usage it wears out. This is called depreciation in accounting procedures; a certain sum is set aside each time period, to allow for the using-up of capital. Money thus marked is not profit; it is representative of that portion of capital used up in the production process. It is necessary to employ an allowance for depreciation in accounting, because the life of capital is frequently longer than the time covered by the accounting period.

It is normally not possible to measure precisely the wear and tear on a machine each year, for example. If, for any reason, depreciation is not considered; if it is understated, or erroneously estimated too low, a situation occurs whereby capital is being consumed. This means new capital is not being formed as fast as existing capital is wearing out. If this should happen in a general way throughout the economy, eventually there would be less capital available than before, with a resultant drop in production.

Present capital in existence today was accumulated in the past. Those who accumulated it yesterday had to judge as best they could in what specific form to make their capital investment; what was considered a good investment at that time may turn out to be a bad investment in the light of today's changed requirements. Nevertheless, the men of today must use the accumulated capital to the best possible advantage, converting it where practical, using it until is wears out where practical and in some cases, abandoning it altogether.

Technological improvements work through capital accumulation to bring about an increase in productivity. These improvements are most often ways of employing more or better capital goods to multiply output; without capital they are of small value, since their use is restricted by the amount of capital available for their implementation.

There are more technological improvements at our disposal than there is capital to effect their use. The "undeveloped" nations of the world are in that predicament for this very reason. Access to processes for increasing production is freely available to these countries (or available at small cost), but technological aid of itself will not make them richer. They must have capital—the factories, machinery, railroads, trained workers, etc.—to utilize such processes. Increased capital allows increased production and increased production leads to increased wealth.

Entrepreneurs Earn Profits and Losses

We have talked about the factors of production—land, labor, and capital—as they exist at the higher levels of production. Yet to be answered is the question of how these factors, in their many possible forms, are brought together into consumers' products.

The unifying, activating force in the market is the desire for profits. The possibility of making profits causes all the factors of production to assume their proper places. Profits, in a generic sense, are the fuel for any economic system; the energizer which keeps it going in the direction of maximum human satisfactions. The absence of profit means that land, labor, and capital are combining so as to diminish human satisfactions; it betokens economic waste or destruction.

Profits, or losses, express the differential between costs of the factors of production used in creating a good or service, and the price it is finally sold for. If the item sells for more than its total production cost, that gain is a *profit;** if it sells for less, it is a loss.

A difficulty involved in the word "profit" is that, being a short and simple word used so frequently, one can be unaware that it has several meanings. When reading economics it is necessary to determine how the word is being used.

"Profit" is used here in its technical sense of "economic profit" as a measuring tool to determine the actual and real overall gain (or loss) ascribable to a particular economic activity. It means whatever is left over after all costs are covered. These include not only the ordinary and usual production and overhead costs, depreciation and obsolence, appropriate reserves, all taxes and wages including management wages, but also a correct allocation for return on equity money invested.

Contrasted to "economic profits" is what might be called "accounting profits" or "net profits" or businessman's profits." These are the figures ordinarily shown on a businessmans profit and loss statement and are the kind the world of commerce works with constantly. An individual businessman has his bookkeeper prepare an income statement at the end of the year. This "accounting profit" supposedly tells him how much he earned or lost, but normally it is not the same as "economic profit". To arrive at "economic profit" for his enterprise it

Individuals who engage in profit-seeking are called entrepreneurs. There are all types of these profit-seekers operating in the market—from the owners of a billion-dollar corporation or the self-employed farmer, to the worker who changes jobs and offers his services in a hopefully better market. Again, we are talking about the economic function such individuals perform. Each acts to obtain a profit for himself, although many (or most) of them may be unaware of playing a part in the broader role of creating consumer goods and services.

The only way an individual entrepreneur can make a profit, however, is by producing something his customer

would be necessary to further refine the "accounting profit" figure by allocations for the businessman's salary (at the going market rate for the service he performs) and for return on money he has invested in the business. Similarly, the bottom line of General Motors Corp. annual report is labeled "net profit" and shows how much money the firm earned for the year. This is a most useful figure to General Motors, but it is not "economic profit" as it does not contain an allocation for return on equity capital invested. "Economic profit" would be the "accounting profit" less whatever its invested equity capital would earn on the open market in a similar risk situation.

The customary "accounting profit" always is higher than the true "economic profit" (as it neglects very real costs.) "Accounting profit" is a useful tool in comparing yearly changes in the same business and is not too misleading in comparing different business since roughly the same costs are omitted. But, "economic profit" not "accounting profit" is the true yardstick of how well an entrepreneur is running his business. The pressure of competition continually presses profits down, so that for the average business in average times "economic profit" tends toward zero.

Profit is the basic guide to all economic activity and it is essential that it be fully and accurately understood.

—and ultimately the consumer—wants, so that the effect of his profit-seeking activity, if correct, is the serving of the consumer. If the entrepreneurial action is incorrect—that is, if he loses money—it is the entrepreneur who takes the direct loss. From the consumer's point of view the enterprise of the entrepreneurs is a case of "Heads I win, tails you lose".

An entrepreneur tries for profits by obtaining several factors of production; then doing something with them to increase their value. He buys with money one or more of the countless factors available. By some such process as adding to, dividing, combining, transporting, storing, etc., he seeks to advance the factors one or several steps nearer to a consumable good.

Because the entrepreneur advances money, those persons engaged in making goods at the higher stages (goods not immediately consumable), can continue to do so; in effect, being paid in consumption goods. In this manner, Jones, our original iron miner, can continue to produce iron ore even though the ore he digs from the ground is worthless as a consumer's product, at that stage. He is paid for his ore in money by an entrepreneur who, by combining it with other labor, capital and land factors, will turn the ore into steel. Steel is not a consumer's product either, and the steel manufacturer sells it for money to another entreprenuer who, by further combination with other factors, will convert the steel product into toasters. Toasters still in the factory are not a consumer good until they have been transported and sold to the retailer, who will see that they finally reach the ultimate user.

In each step of the process, the entrepreneur has advanced money (present goods) in exchange for raw or partially finished goods, with expectation of adding to the value of the goods and re-selling them for more money later.

The consumer demand for toasters works back along the process we have just outlined to make its influence felt in these higher stages. The entrepreneur, in striving for profits, attempts to arrange the production process—hence, the factors of production—in such a way as to best satisfy consumer demands. He is the agent of the consumer. He bids for goods of the higher orders, and a demand-supply relationship is set up exactly as on the consumer level, with all its attendant fluctuations.

However, the entrepreneur is always limited in what he can correctly pay for the factors of production, as he can never afford to pay more than will be refunded to him by the consumers who buy the finished product. By putting differing ceilings on what an entrepreneur can bid for the factors of production, the consumer forces these goods of the higher orders to go to that entrepreneur whose products he most desires.

Some people would say that books on economics are more important than comic books, but so long as consumers support the publishers of comic books by buying more comics than economic treatises, those publishers will be able to bid for and buy more of the same paper, ink, labor, etc., used in the production of both. The consumer has simply decided he prefers comic books; and the entrepreneur is helpless before such demand, regardless of his personal tastes. He will continue to put out more comic books than books about economics, because that is what the consumer wants.

Thus, it is through profits that the entrepreneur is able to gauge whether or not he is supplying the wants of the consumer. If a profit is being made, he is clearly doing so because he is able not only to recoup the cost of the item he is producing, but an additional amount as well. If he is losing money, it is equally manifest that other, better uses can be made of the factors of production he is incorrectly converting.

The pressure is always on the entrepreneur to seek out better utilization of the factors of production. He must judge the state of affairs existing in the market and act accordingly; in so doing, he is always concerned with the future demands of the consumer.

The past is gone, the present is being take care of; the entrepreneur must plan for the future. He must project the future state of the market—its demands, the factors of production which will be available, his ability to correlate them—and reduce it all to terms of dollars and cents. Since the future is uncertain, the entrepreneur cannot be sure his plans will be successful; but if the future were known, then everyone would be prepared—so there would be no chance for profits.

Through the process which rewards the best estimates with profits, the most consistenly successful entrepreneur continues in business, while his less artful colleagues fall by the wayside. In such a manner, the crucial and difficult task of anticipating the future comes to rest in the hands of the entrepreneur who has been most successful in the past; and to the extent he is prepard by such experience to project the future, the consumer is best served.

The role of an entrepreneur is most dramatic and exciting when he is bringing to the market a new product— that is, one which the consumer himself is not yet aware he wants.

Henry Ford had to obtain the factors necessary to make his automobile without having any way of knowing, except by educated guess, whether the consumers—most of whom had never heard of such a contraption—would buy enough of his cars to return his investment, plus a profit. Many people at the time did not share his vision, and refused to invest in automobiles. In retrospect, the successful outcome seems obvious and the correct decision clearcut. (The decisions are always obvious to Monday morning quarterbacks.)

Let us say that Smith, the shoemaker, is considering the manufacture of house slippers. He surveys the market and interprets it in light of his knowledge and experience. He knows the price of the various kinds of leather; he knows the price of wool; and he also knows the price of labor.

These costs, as well as the prices of many other factors he will need in the manufacturing process, are known to him because each factor is presently being used in the market and there is a demand and supply relationship established for it. He then assesses what he assumes will be the demand for the kind of house slipper he has in mind; if he finds the results to his liking he will purchase the necessary factors and begin production of house slippers.

At this point he has already decided between leather and wool house slippers on the basis of the particular cost and probable demand for each. If Smith is able to sell the slippers at a profit, he has forecast correctly and knows he is doing the right thing in making these kind of slippers at this price. The customers approve. If he suffers a loss on the operation instead, it means he is not doing the right thing from the viewpoint of the consumer, who do not desire to buy this type slipper at this price, as much as they desire something else. Smith will get out of the house slipper business and both he and the consumer will be happier—Smith, because he no longer is losing money and the consumer, because additional factors will not be going into these slippers, but into a commodity they prefer.

From the foregoing discussion of profits, we can see that, just as there is no such thing as a fair or just price, there is also no such thing as a fair or just profit. Profits are simply the difference between cost and selling price, and could vary in each and every situation. The reason there is no such variation in profit is because, as men become more adept at their business practices, competition acts as a great leveler.

Profits tend to move toward an equilization; over the long haul they mainly benefit the workers. As was pointed out in the section concerning capital, this factor flows toward the higher profit areas. Also, as would be expected, entrepreneurs themselves tend to move into higher profit areas, and neglect the lower. The result of such action is increased production in higher profit areas, decreased production in lower profit areas, and a consequent tendency toward equilization of the profit rates throughout the economy.

An illustration will show how this equilization occurs. Let us take the case of Mr. Green, who has accumulated some capital and has invested in a new labor-saving machine which, by employing fewer workers, is able to turn out aspirin tablets at one-half the cost of previous methods. Green decides to sell his aspirin for enough under the going price to have a large market, but at a price where he can still make a hefty profit.

As soon as the aspirins come on the market, everyone benefits by having aspirin available at less cost. Soon others —seeing Green's success—will begin to use the same methods, and the competitive process will lower the price of aspirin still further until entrepreneurial return becomes similar to other ventures. The consumers will have the extra money they have saved (in buying the lower priced aspirin), to spend for something else. The demand for these other goods then bids up the prices being asked for them, and draws people to work to fill the new demand.

In the meantime, Green must dispose of his profits and no matter how he elects to do this—whether by enlarging his aspirin business, investing in another business, or just spending the money on himself—in so doing, he increases the demand for someone else's goods or services. In turn, the recipient of Green's new demand is able to increase the demand for additional goods or services, and so on, through the interrelated process.

All production requires labor. As new production is called forth to meet the increased demand (caused both by Green's disposition of profits, and the consumers, who were able to effect savings in their aspirin purchases), workers see the demand for their services bid up, with accompaning wage raises. They are the final, major recipients of Green's profits and innovation.

Green has simply increased production. This is how wealth is created and when wealth is created everyone shares in it. If the entrepreneur makes a profit as a reward for creating wealth at his own financial risk—while at the same time serving the consumer—none but the purblind would say his profits were evil.

The title of this chapter is "The Production Story" and we have been discussing what the factors of production are, and how they are combined into creating want-satisfying goods and services. We can now see more clearly the interdependence and cohesiveness of the economic processsess, for we have, at the same time, been speaking of individual carnings, as indicated by the sub-topics:

"Land Earns Rent";

"Labor Earns Wages";

"Capital Earns Interest";

"Entrepreneurs Earn Profits and Losses".

Thus, while answering the question, *"What will be produced?"*, we have simultaneously answered the questions, *"By whom?"* and *"For whom?"*.

Chapter 7

MARKET ORGANIZATION

The Selective Process

Where men are free to choose, they choose whatever they consider best for themselves. In *Consumers' Capitalism*, this individual selective action drives the market toward equilibrium—but it is an equilibrium destined never to be reached. The same freedom which pushes the market in this direction also allows men to change their minds; and changes mean new conditions, with new routes to follow to accommodate those new conditions.

Within the market structure of *Consumers' Capitalism*, there is utmost freedom of opportunity. This freedom does not entitle everyone to be seven feet tall, evenly muscled, and handsome of face. It means there is equal opportunity for serving the consumer to the extent of each individual capability; and to benefit accordingly.

We have seen that the worker must tailor his own desire to consumer demand, if he wishes to take advantage of higher paying jobs; that the owner of capital must take care to invest in enterprises which will provide what the consumers want, in order to maintain and increase his capital; that the entrepreneur must be on the lookout for ever better ways to utilize the factors of production.

Men, using these opportunities, cause the tendency toward equilibrium in the market. Loan money flows to wherever the return is likely to be greatest, with resulting interest rates which become more nearly equal. Entrepreneurs seek the highest profit areas; thus profits tend to level out. Workers, in leaving lesser paying jobs for better paying ones, cause wage rates to achieve a closer degree of parity.

This is a continuous, on-flowing process and no one can rest upon previously-won acclaim for long. The task of consumer satisfaction begins afresh, each day in the market place. Consumers are notoriously capricious, flocking to those producers who offer what they want; then, as wants change, seeking other sources. On such a foundation, no economic caste system can be erected or maintained; individuals are constantly moving up and down the ladder of financial success. There is always room at the top, room at the bottom, and room everywhere else along the scale. Just as in the social world, where no man can force another to like him; in *Consumers' Capitalism*, no man may force another to do business with him. His economic success depends upon how well he can convince others his product or service fills their need.

Human relationships, working toward harmony, exist to the limit of the *Consumers' Capitalism* market. If this system were practiced on a worldwide basis the tendency toward equilibrium would be worldwide also. If practiced in a single country, the tendency toward equality would at least exist within that country.

The drive toward equilibrium explains why people and industries locate where they do. Unhindered, men go where the opportunity is most attractive. Fertile lands will draw men to use them; natural resources will attract men to develop them; capital, left in a certain place by past generations, will be utilized there.

To some individuals, a propensity to live in a certain area may represent a special kind of return not measurable in monetary value, and people may therefore accept lower wages in this area; but this, too, represents what these people consider their best opportunity. Because of this search for opportunity, prices for the same goods tend to remain constant in differing geographic locations thoughout the market with only a transportation differential, where it is applicable.

Size of Firms

As part of the general tendency toward equilibrium, brought on by equal opportunities, there is a tendency for each firm, operating in *Consumers' Capitalism,* to move toward the size at which it realizes maximum profits. In this instance, the uniformity the market seeks is one of maximum profits rather than physical or financial magnitude, and thus to say that a firm is too big or too small is meaningless. In a highly specialized world, these relative terms cannot be applied on the basis of physical size, number of workers employed, gross business, or similar factors.

The mass production of motor cars cannot be done by a small entrepreneur, working in his garage. Rather, it requires a tremendous investment in capital and the efforts of thousands (or hundreds of thousands) of people to produce cars at popular prices. If, however, we are talking about the manufacture of pin cushions, a different set of standards will apply.

Firms have a certain portion of costs which do not vary directly with each additional unit of output. These are called fixed costs or general overhead, in accounting terms. Each firm ideally utilizes these expenses to the greatest extent by spreading them as far as they can over output, which serves to increase profits. A producer of automobiles must have a large plant with sufficient machinery and workers, in order to make just one automobile. He can make the second automobile at less cost; the third at still less; etc.

Beyond the general principle of maximizing profits, economics cannot say what the correct size should be for a firm, and to prescribe certain physical dimensions would certainly be impossible. This is one decision which businessmen must make on the merits of each specific case. It is often difficult for the businessman to determine just what the proper size of his company should be—until his customers supply a clue.

A similar question relates to the number of firms operating within a particular field. Here again, economic theory can give no concrete answer which could possibly apply in each case. The answer depends upon the size of the existing firms in the field, the size of the market, and the many variables inherent in each situation.

Companies can buy out their suppliers or set up their own sub-companies for supply purposes. (An example of such vertical integration would be that of an auto manufacturer, who produces the tires he uses on his cars.) When the specifics of each case are such that formation of sub-companies results in greater profits, companies will be encouraged to do this. In operating these supply divisions, however, managers check the division's results against those of similar, independent companies operating in the market. If the division is not paying its own way, the company is not maximizing its profits, but losing part of them. In this way, supply divisions within a large company are, in effect, made to compete in the market as realistically as if they were actually out looking for customers.

Big firms, as well as small, can go bankrupt in *Consumers Capitalism*. Size is no protection whatever from the market. A company grows large and stays that way only if it continues to provide what people want. Big firms are a monument to success, but a shaky monument at best. If, tomorrow, nobody buys their product, they will soon be gone. A big firm (or any firm in *Consumers' Capitalism*), is charged each and every moment with pleasing its customers at least as well as—or better than—competing firms; failure to do so will lead to insolvency.

In an increasingly specialized and technically complex society some firms turn to various forms of publicity to make themselves known throughout the market. One such media is advertising, which is frequently accused of somehow manipulating people into buying something they don't want. If the present state of knowledge is such that science is hard put to describe the reasons men smoke cigarettes, it is even harder pressed to explain why some men prefer Cigarette *A* to Cigarette *B*.

From the economic point of view, Cigarette *A* and Cigarette *B* can represent to an individual two distinct categories of consumer goods; in exercising the freedom which is his in the market place, he chooses the one he prefers, or none. Printed words or catchy songs cannot force him to do something he does not want to do. If this were not true, the makers of Pierce-Arrows, Packards, Edsels, and Studebakers would still happily be in business.

All advertising can do is inform the buyer something about products which are available in the market; and to the extent that buyers are better informed, they are better able to discriminate as to which products will meet their requirements.

Monopoly

A great deal has been written about monopoly in economic activity. In fact, so much alarm has been created in popular journals that the subject is often clouded in emotionalism, rather than scrutinized in the light of accurate analysis.

To begin, we must define the term, monopoly. By one definition, a monopoly is said to exist when there is only one seller in a market. This is so-called "pure" monopoly. In actuality, this situation prevails throughout *Consumers' Capitalism*. Each man, in a free state, is the owner of his own labor and property.

By this definition, then, everyone becomes a monopolist. The worker holds a monopoly on his labor; the store keeper, on his merchandise; the farmer, on his land; etc. A worker may perform an individualistic and specialized service which cannot be duplicated (only Frank Sinatra can sing songs sung by Frank Sinatra). A store keeper may own the only grocery store, in a town or neighborhood too small to support another; he is the only outlet in that market. Is the answer, then, to nationalize Frank Sinatra and the corner grocer, in order to prevent monopoly?

Such obvious inconsistencies lead critics to concentrate, instead, on monopoly prices. It is not monopoly, per se, which is bad, the argument goes, but monopoly prices.

"Monopoly prices" has come to mean a price arising from a situation where a seller has banded together with other sellers who are producing the same product, to sell this product for a higher unit price than could be asked under more competitive conditions. "Monopoly prices" denotes some kind of imperfect competition, where sellers get their own price without regard for market forces.

Such a definition of monopoly prices is an example of circular reasoning. If there is a monopoly selling goods at monopoly prices, then there is no way of objectively determining what the competitive price would be in the market; hence there would be no way of knowing whether the so-called monopoly price is really that at all.

The fallacy in applying this sort of a definition to actual cases can be seen through observation of the U.S. Government's action in anti-trust cases. A firm has been known to be prosecuted for selling at prices which are too low, an allegation which hints at a conspiracy to monopolize, by putting others out of business through underselling them; others have been prosecuted for selling at prices which are too high, which allegedly means the firm in question is charging monopoly prices; still others have been charged with selling at the same price, which the government sees as collusion and monopoly.

Consumer Protection

In *Consumers' Capitalism*, the possibility of a seller, or group of sellers, consciously and consistently acting in a manner contrary to the aggregate wishes of the consumers, is practically negligible. The seller cannot charge any price he fancies, because competition always moves the market in the direction of consumer satisfaction. Where there is no hindrance, and men are free to engage in competition, no person (or persons) is free from market influences.

If a seller entirely controls a particular product, and attempts to charge prices which return high profits, such action is like waving a red flag in front of a bull. The high profits act like a magnet—drawing entrepreneurs, workers, and capital into the field to partake of the profits.

A seller may attempt to drive other sellers out of the market by underselling them, with the idea of charging high prices when he is alone in the field, but if he is successful, and begins charging these high prices (thereby reaping high profits), competition is again attracted, so he is back where he started.

If a seller dominates or partially controls the field, his attempt to charge high prices and reap high profits will not only draw new competition, but the bigger profits will also increase the growth of the smaller firms operating in that area, causing them to become a source of increased competition.

If a group of firms band together and attempt to control prices by way of a cartel or pool agreement the biggest profits go to the firms in the cartel which are the most efficient producers. Under a pool arrangement no individual firm can expand very much, since the essence of a cartel is a pro-rata sharing of the market. Unfettered, the more efficient firms could do better; being the best producers they have nothing to fear from the market, and their presence in the cartel actually serves to keep alive their inefficient counterparts. For this reason all such "monopoly" agreements, when based only upon mutual consent, are unstable and tend to break up.

A would-be monopolist not only has to contend with the direct competition his high profits will attract, but with competition through substitution as well. This is especially important in cases where the monopolized product is a natural resource, but is true elsewhere as well. (What would happen, if someone should gain control of all the copper mines in the world?)

In a free market, price determination is an intersection where demand and supply meet. If the price is made artificially higher in some manner, less will be used; as the price goes up, demand goes down, and if the price is fixed extremely high, very little will be bought at all. Price is the determinate of how much any item will be used. In a specialized and technical economy, this elasticity of demand will be magnified by the ready substitution of one item for another.

Science has become so proficient in developing new products that there are very few items for which a more or less satisfactory substitute is not available. How satisfactory the substitute is, depends upon the relationship of its price and utility to that of the original item.

This type of contest is continually being waged in our modern markets. Thus, the makers of aluminum, steel, glass and plastics, are involved in trying to win the food and beverage container market. In this case, they are not concerned about raising their prices, but rather, lowering them in an effort to capture a larger portion of this market. Copper producers, whose product has had a history of violent price fluctuations, have seen how a fractional rise in the price of copper sends former users to other metals and plastics. Their concern is for lower or stabilized prices, not higher ones. If someone owned all the copper mines, and attempted to raise prices, he would soon discover that for all practical purposes he had been bypassed in the market place.

Given the almost limitless arrangements possible for factors of production, it can be expected that, from time to time, one producer will develop some happy combination which will allow better production at lower cost. In this circumstance, the larger these efficient firms grow, the more people they are serving, and serving better. New firms grow into giants; and these giants die off and disappear as one or another move to an advanced position in the race.

The money winners in open competition can never relax on past victories, because the contest is endless; with the rest of the field (both real and potential) forever snapping at their heels. The entreprenurial function is planning for the future; therefore, a firm that today holds a dominant position must mind its laurels, to maintain its place. To a forward-looking businessman, smaller firms and new firms entering the field represent a source of possible, strong future competition. A dominant giant is unlikely to laugh off a competitive challenge simply because, at the moment, the challenger's penetration of the market seems insignificant.

The unrelenting competition which protects the customers may be hidden just below the surface of business activity, since it can occur in areas other than dollars and cents selling prices. There may be strong, competitive innovation between producers—each attempting to bring out something new and better at the same price, or even at a price slightly lower, or higher.

There may be competition in service or availability. This kind of competition, plus out-and-out price competition, causes an expanding economy to proliferate the outpouring of kinds, types, quantities, and qualities of goods offered to the consumer; putting the customer in an even better position to bargain with his suppliers.

So far we have been discussing monopoly and other such facets of economic activity as they would appear in a system of *Consumers' Capitalism*, where there is unhindered and free expression of value choices. If the conditions are such that there is hindrance, and choices are not free—or only partially so—these described states of affairs would not exist. They would be changed, or altered. (The alterations will be examined in the succeeding chapters.)

Part III
BUREAUCRATIC CAPITALISM

Chapter 8

ANOTHER METHOD OF PROBLEM-SOLVING

Appeal of Utopia

In previous chapters it has been shown how, in a system of Consumers' Capitalism, individual man can better arrange his personal well-being, if he so chooses, by serving others; and to the extent he can provide what other people want his own economic prosperity can be increased. It has been further shown how individuals, acting in this manner increase the general prosperity through the sum of their productive efforts. This is not regarded as a satisfactory state of affairs by some people, who have proposed an alternate way to answer the basic economic question. "Who produces what, for whom?"

A discussion concerning why some men reject the idea of *Consumers' Capitalism,* and the principle of free choice

119

which accompanies it, does not come under the heading
of economics but rather involves studies such as philosophy, psychology, and history. Nevertheless, it will be
helpful to mention (as background for developing the
description of *Bureaucratic Capitalism*) some of the more
popular reasons given for rejecting the system of *Consumers' Capitalism.*

Some men consider themselves at odds with *Consumers'
Capitalism,* when actually they do not understand what
it is. It cannot be said they reject it outright, since by
definition it is impossible to reject something of which
one knows nothing.

Many resent the fact that in economic activity some
men are superior to others. This kind of thinking defies
reason; actually our eternal thanks should go to the great
minds and abilities of superior men who have so enriched
the lives of us all. The dull, ambitionless laborer, who
resents the fact that all men do not operate on his low
level, should rather be grateful. It is because of men on
the higher level of achievement that his own struggle for
livelihood is rewarded far beyond his own powers of
creation.

Some men regard the necessity of working for a living
as a mean trick, played upon them, not by nature, but by
their fellow man. A few people expect a world of eternal
paradise to be theirs for the taking—in which food, clothing, all necessities, and luxuries flow down from the sky
borne upon a wish; most are not so fanciful, knowing only

their own struggle, and believing the next fellow is not struggling so hard as they, but is nevertheless getting more in return. To such luckless individuals, it seems that the "rich" don't work (or work less), yet have abundance. Is this just? How much more fair it would be if everybody had the same amount! "To each according to his need; *from* each according to his ability!" Unfortunately, the overlooked difficulty of this catch-phrase is that often those who utter it the loudest assume they should be the ones who determine their own needs.

At this point, we have come a full 180° turn from *Consumers' Capitalism,* which is a system where individuals pursuing economic success are called upon to serve others. Instead, we have a system where others are called upon to serve the individual. The individual seeks to impress his value choice upon others.

By pseudo-intellectual process, this idea may be carried to the heights of altruism—which, nonetheless, cannot mask the truth. A person may say, "My needs are many, and I want others to provide them for me." Or, he may say, "My needs are few, but I want the world's goodies to be shared by (choose one):

a. the masses,
b. the majority,
c. society,
d. my race,
e. my country,
f. [ad infinitum]".

Any such statement is an attempt by one individual to set his own value judgments as a standard for others to follow.

From this kind of thinking, the idea of economic equality sprang forth. It began by being expressed in the communistic manner of dividing the existing wealth among everyone; but the technicalities of the world soon bypassed this idea. The obvious advantages of mass production, carried on in giant factories and spread through mass distribution, made it impractical to divide the world's riches on a share-for-share basis. To revolt by taking home from the factory one's spin-nut inspection machine would be useless. It would be better, it was argued, to make use of the highly productive set-ups by leaving them intact, and receiving their advantages. It would only be necessary to make sure the output was parcelled out correctly. Therefore it should be socialized—belonging to society, produced for society, and divided among the members of society.

The most magnetic slogan in human history was issued. *"Workers of the world unite—you have nothing to lose but your chains."* It fell as a blinding stroke of righteousness in an evil world, upon men convinced of the unfairness of life. Here at last was a way to make everyone truly and finally equal, a way to extend value choices to the whole of humanity. Here at last was the inevitable higher order on the road to utopia.

The Selling Job

In a free system man has no way—other than persuasion

—to influence another man's value judgments. However, if one man has superior force at his disposal he can dominate a weaker individual, forcing the other to agree with him—or else. In terms of the modern make-up of countries, this control shows itself through police and army action. Those in charge of these establishments have a lever with which to control the economic value choices of others.

That this possible domination exists, does not necessarily mean it will be used. Police and armies originated as specialized organizations, for protecting those who supported them. Within a free system, this is the limit of their function. In some nations of the contemporary world who seek to move toward a system of *Bureaucratic Capitalism*, however, the power of the police and army has been turned to calling the economic tune, as some try to force their value choices upon others. This has been done through the magic of one hypnotic, enticing, all-encompassing word.

That word is *planning*.

It is said that the market system is not planned, and an alternate system to solve the economic problems would be both planned and coordinated; thus, more efficient. No more helter-skelter guesswork with resultant errors and mistakes. If it is demonstratively, unmistakenly possible for an individual shoe factory to plan its production in such a manner as to increase output, then planning should be expanded to include the whole of the economy, and to increase the output of the entire economy. The basic fallacy involved here is the assumption that in a market system economic activity is unplanned.

A goodly number of pages in this book have been devoted to explaining how *Consumers' Capitalism* is just the opposite of an unplanned system—rather, it is planned, but with an important difference. It is planned by the consumers.

We have seen how the consumers control and direct value choices up and down the line of production, and that they determine not only who makes what, but also how it is to be divided. When a person rejects the supposedly unplanned state of *Consumers' Capitalism,* what he is really rejecting is the fact that it is planned according to an aggregate of consumer desires, rather than his own.

In *Consumers' Capitalism,* there may or may not be available free lunches, high quality ballet, or any of a thousand and one things a particular individual might desire. But the non-availability of these special items does not mean the system is not planned; it means only that it is not planned in the manner in which the dissenting individual thinks it ought to be.

The concept of planning is important in *Bureaucratic Capitalism,* because when enough people agree economic activity should be *planned,* control of the police and army are put into the hands of the planners so they will have the power to enforce their plans.

Because men have a desire to express their own value choices within the economic realm, the idea of planning must be sold, and necessarily sold in disguise. The word *planning* (as it is used with regard to *Bureaucratic Capitalism*) means directing the economy into different channels than it would normally take. (It is totally without meaning to speak of planning something which would occur regardless.) *Planning* therefore means forcing people to do something on an economic level which they otherwise would not do, and this is the reason why planned economics *always* involves force and coercion.

Planning implies not only planners, but the individual planning for his own utopia. One must plan for something. It is by presenting economic theory as a means for attaining one's goals that the idea of planning is made palatable. Few planners would expect to have a following if they stood up and declared: "You do not know what food to eat or clothes to wear, nor where to live; but I know what you should eat and wear, and where you should live, so I will direct you in these activities." Rather, some abstraction is held up, as the ideal to which individuals should be subordinated.

This ideal is often conveyed through use of the word, "Society"; and the proposition is stated thus: "Individual man is unimportant; he is only a little cog in the vast complex of Society. Society is the human reality, and it is only through Society that the individual can have any meaning; therefore, we must plan and work for Society."

On occasion, as fits the circumstances, Race, Nation, Our Children, Our Grandchildren, Our Way of Doing Things, etc., may be substituted for Society. Once the idea of the primacy of Society, Race, or Nation is sold, it is then necessary only to complete the pattern by identifying Society with The State; and a firm foundation for the "Dictatorship of the Proletariat" has thus been established. The chief planner becomes the functioning State because he is the State; he is also Society and he acts in the name of the State and Society.

Those individuals who do not see their duty to Society and the State as the director sees it are prodded—by bayonet if need be—into that mode of activity the director has determined as being beneficial to his concept of Society and the State. Any persons unwilling to comply with the wishes of the director must be administered suitable reminders; if this is not sufficient, they must be eliminated entirely as being guilty of anti-social behavior.

How It Works

A nation may move toward a system of *Bureaucratic Capitalism* (or Socialism) through various means. The two best-known are the Communist (or Russian) variety, and the German (or Fascist) type. In the Communist system, the state owns all property outright. The same effect is achieved in the German or Fascist type by placing nominal control of property into the hands of individuals, but actual control with the State. How the system comes into being—whether revolution, evolution, the Divine Right of Kings, armed occupation, or free election—and what a system calls itself, is not pertinent to economic analysis. A nation is determined to be *Bureaucratic Capitalistic,* or partially so, by the way in which it is organized to answer the basic economic questions.

Bureaucratic Capitalism occurs when the economic decisions are made by a Bureaucrat (or Bureaucrats), and these decisions are backed by force. Certain characteristics emerge as a corollary of this mode of social organization, and are indicative of the nature of *Bureaucratic Capitalism;* they are all concerned with lessening the freedom of an individual to act in the economic sphere, with correspondent lessening of restraints imposed upon that power which the Bureaucrats may exercise over others. Most essentially, private property as an individual right must be done away with completely. Individuals cannot freely act to dispose of their property, while directors simultaneously control it.

The chief director has control of the entire economy. Because of the multi-level nature of modern economic activity, it is often necessary that he delegate some of his authority to lesser Bureaucrats. Acting with him, they plan production and consumption activity, decide which factors of production will be devoted to which items, and who will receive them for consumption.

If they wish to engage in capital accumulation to increase later production, they simply designate a certain portion of current production to this purpose. If they wish to have a nation of wood-cutters, workingmen, or warriors, they direct the populace to fill these kinds of jobs. If they want a different geographic distribution of population, or a different production balance, they shift whatever and whomever they wish, in order to attain it. So long as they control the police and army, they need not be concerned about the consequences of their activity —short of a general revolution.

Within such a system the bureaucratic decisions become economic reality. The Bureaucrats decide what is good, what is bad, what is worthwhile, and what is not. For a graphic illustration, consider the story of the Moscow Cable Factory, and how it was able to reduce its copper consumption by economizing its operation. As a result of its efficiency, the factory was fined for not meeting its scrap quota!

Such events are not uncommon in a system of *Bureaucratic Capitalism*. The Bureaucrats decide what is useful production, what is scrap, and which should be produced. If they have authority to do so, it follows in perfectly logical fashion that they may emphasize scrap production if they wish.

In dealing with other nations of the world through international trade, the Bureaucrats' whims are not supreme; they must conduct themselves according to the terms and conditions of the international market if they want to do business there. Free men will not willingly pay $1.00 for an item which can be bought elsewhere for 50¢, regardless of the Bureaucrats' desire.

To whatever extent a *Bureaucratic Capitalist* nation engages in international trade, and that trade is free, the Bureaucrat must tailor his domestic economy to the international market. Thus the Bureaucrats tend to shy away from such limits to their power. Except when moved by overriding political reasons, *Bureaucratic Capitalist* nations are hesitant to engage in international trade. One method of gauging the amount of *Bureaucratic Capitalism* existing in a nation, is to examine its standings in international trade statistics (not counting the somewhat primitive, barter-type transactions with other *Bureaucratic Capitalistic* countries.)

Other things being equal, those economies which are more inclined to *Bureaucratic Capitalism*, trade less on the international market. Individual businessmen in freer countries look longingly at the *Bureaucratic Capitalistic* market—there are so many things their people want, and need. But is is a one-way street. The Bureaucrats, operating as they do in a partial vacuum, have very little to sell at competitive prices.

Chapter 9

UTOPIA AS IT CAME TO BE

The Trouble Was

However inviting and beautiful the socialistic utopia was from a philosophical or psychological point of view, there was one overwhelming flaw in its economic theory which doomed it to a perpetual and dismal failure. It didn't correspond with the real world.

The theory of society owning the means of production, with society producing the most needed goods; and of society consuming goods equitably, was a delightful abstraction, so long as it was left hanging in the air and was not questioned. The evils this system was supposedly designed to correct were held to be of such a pressing nature that people didn't inquire into the proposed cure. But others did begin asking questions.

Society is a term which is useful only within a narrow, well-defined context. It means a group, classified by means of certain common characteristics. Society, as a group, does not produce. Society, as a group, does not consume. It is the individual within the group who produes and consumes.

In this method of economic problem-solving individual selection of what to produce and consume has already been ruled out. Such a system is *Consumers' Capitalism*, to which we are presently discussing an alternative. Hence, the unanswerable question arises: if individual selection is not considered, how are individuals in Society (the group) going to know what to produce and what to consume?

To which is answered: "Society will be guided by those who know best—*The Specialists. The Master Planners.*"

But this is not really an answer; it is only taking a general question and serving it up to some specific persons —in this case, the Master Planners. How are the Master Planners to know which economic paths to follow?

Suppose that in the socialist utopia, the most able individuals assume the responsibility of directing the production and consumption cycle. It might be that these individuals are godlike in perfection—always acting within the sphere of their mandate—and further, that their mandate may be the greatest possible production/consumption for everyone. Suppose that the entire population may be convinced of the rightness of the system, and cooperate fully with the Master Planner.

Still, even when the best possible conditions are met, there remains the unanswerable question. The Master Planner is still an individual human being, not gifted with omnipotence or omniscience. Without a market to guide him, he has no possible way of knowing how to arrange the factors of production in the most efficient manner; he has only his own whim. Indeed, "most efficient manner" becomes a meaningless phrase.

Economic goods are scarce; the production of Item *A* means that at the same time, and with the same raw materials, Item *B cannot* be produced. In *Consumers' Capitalism,* the relationship between economic goods is established by individuals bidding in the market for those goods they consider worthwhile; it is because of this defined relationship of value that men can calculate that which is economically expedient. In *Bureaucratic Capitalism,* where there is no market to establish the relative value of goods, no such calculation is possible.

If, in the Socialist utopia, the Master Planner decides to make house slippers, he has no way of knowing whether to make them from wool or from leather. In *Consumers' Capitalism,* the price of both commodities are known, as well as the price of all factors which contribute to their manufacture. The price of leather is ultimately influenced by the price of filet mignon, the price of cattle feed, and the prices of countless other items. These prices— which influence the price of leather—are themselves determined in a similar way, by an almost infinite series of market-place happenings. The same is true of wool. The resultant prices are the data which men have to work with, to guide them in what they do.

In the Socialist system, there are no such guides. Before the Planner can decide to make his house slippers from leather, he must determine the value of leather as compared to wool; the solving of this problem in turn, opening an endless, retrogressive, stream of questions which no Planner, even if aided by a multitude of Sub-Planners and computers, can answer. He can only decide by whim.

Moreover, whatever production figures the Master Planner accomplishes as a result of his whims, the calculations will represent an achievement only to him and to those few who happen—by chance—to agree with him.

The Colossal Failure

Bureaucratic Capitalism (Socialism) is unworkable in theory and, as would be expected, equally unworkable when men attempt to put it into practice. The lofty aims of plenty and equality it so loudly proclaims are never quite achieved. Rather, in direct proportion to the amount of *Bureaucratic Capitalism* involved, there is hardship and misery. When value choices are made by a few Bureaucrats, instead of by individuals acting in a free manner, and when one all-encompassing state monopoly is created, such a system can lead in no other direction than poverty.

Sooner or later, a conflict between the Bureaucrats and

the consumers must arise over what is worthwhile, and the Bureaucrats must resolve this conflict by armed force. The leitmotif of a functioning system of *Bureaucratic Capitalism* becomes the secret police and torture chamber; while slave labor camps become instruments for expediting economic policy. The leaders may speak loftily of planning production for human need, but in the final analysis it is not really production which is planned. Production is inanimate. It is people—not production—who must be forced into channels they have not chosen.

This pattern can be observed in those nations best known for their *Bureaucratic Capitalist* systems. After a long and herioc struggle upward toward a more decent life, men in these countries have again been saddled with slavery, serfdom, and starvation of the masses. Nations become giant tribes, trading with each other by barter (if at all), and every other tribe is suspect. Parts of the world become giant concentration camps, ringed by land mines, with police dogs patrolling the exits.

The necessity for having an economic system which is even partially effective causes the Bureaucrats, from the beginning, to adopt parts of the market system to their needs. We can watch this being done by examining the history of the Soviet Union, the most famous and lengthy example of a nation dedicated to *Bureaucratic Capitalism*.

When the Communists first came to power they proceeded, along good doctrinaire lines, to do away with private trade; they enforced equal earnings, seized whatever they wished, and ruled the entire economy. Thereafter, agricultural output halved, and industrial production nosedived. Lenin instituted "reforms," permitted some private trade, stablized the ruble, let the peasants keep a little of what they grew, and varied pay scales. It is interesting to note that the keystone socialists' concept of equality of income has since been abandoned altogther, and there is presently a great difference in wage rates within the Soviet Union.

As time went on, these and other practicalities of the market system were put to use in the Soviet Union, until by 1962 the Russians had become quite open in their copying of techniques. In that year, a Russian economics professor, Yevsy Liberman, said publicly that the Russian system was inefficient, because it had no way of measuring efficiency. He went on to say that the best way of gauging efficiency was by whether or not an enterprise showed a profit.

"Libermanism," the current name for the practice of using free market principles in the Soviet Union, continues apace. In 1964, *Pravda* editorializes ". . . don't belittle the important role of profit in evaluating and stimulating the work of enterprises . . ." Again in 1964, *Izvestia,* commenting on an experiment in two textile plants, designed to make them operate in a manner similar to plants in a freer market, says, "Russian consumers will obtain a better deal by gaining a larger voice in what kind of goods are produced."

However, the factor which allowed Bureaucratic economics to work as well as they did was not the portions of *Consumers' Capitalism* they adopted (under the guise of "Libermanism" or some other title). These policies helped, but were hamstrung in their effectiveness by contradictory policies.

The saving grace lay in the fact that there were countries where *Consumers' Capitalism* was at least partially operable, and the Bureaucrats could use these economies as models from which to copy. In these nations (and in the world market caused by their trading), prices are established for wool, leather, and all other economic goods.. The Bureaucrats are thereby provided with both a starting point and reference point, and are able to proceed with their own calculations. Without this base they would be helplessly lost in a maze with no beginning nor end.

This can be seen in the Russian economic pronouncements. After almost half a century of experience with their system, they still can speak only in terms of "catching up," "equalling," or "surpassing" the production of the United States in steel, cars, shoes, or space travel.

The Soviets have no way of objectively determining their optimum shoe production. Is it one pair per person? Six pair? Twelve pair? And if this is not known, how does one know when to stop making shoes, and start making something else?

The Bureaucrat's proclivity, politics, or an office dart board, are all equally valid ways of deciding within such a system. It is assumed that the United States has this information, and so the Bureaucrats seek to emulate or surpass the United States in production of economic goods of all types. With this assumption they unknowingly pay the highest compliment to *Consumers' Capitalism*. If the Soviet method, or any such variation of *Bureaucratic Capitalism*, were universally adopted, there would be no models to copy, no patterns from which to judge, and a resulting economic never-never-land, where down is up and up is down.

Part IV

THE BEST OF BOTH ?

Chapter 10

THE MIXED ECONOMY

The Middle Way

In Part I, we talked about the background for economics and the questions any economic system must answer. In Part II, we described one method for answering these questions, called *Consumers' Capitalism;* in Part III, we discussed still another alternative, namely *Bureaucratic Capitalism.*

At last, we are ready to examine the way in which the economic question, "Who produces What, for Whom?" is answered by most of the civilized nations of the world, at the present time.

We may seem to have followed a circuitous route, in order to finally get down to brass tacks and discuss current economic practice; but this has been necessary because most contemporary economic systems are combinations of both *Consumers' Capitalism* and *Bureaucratic Capitalism* mixed together; without understanding each, as it stands alone, we cannot hope to understand the mixture of the two.

On one hand, it has come to be generally recognized that an unadulterated system of *Bureaucratic Capitalism* is unworkable both in theory and practice—as was shown in the preceding section. On the other hand, even the most ardent anti-free-market spokesman must concede that *Consumers' Capitalism* has certain incomparable advantages (especially in the "practical areas") as a means of achieving greater production. Even so, it is claimed that the workability of *Consumers' Capitalism* is not enough; that it can work *too well,* in the *wrong* direction. After all, it may be argued, economics does not set ends or assess human values, nor is it supposed to.

From this point of view, perhaps what is needed is a system which makes use of the advantages of *Consumers' Capitalism,* but channels it in the "proper" directions. *Consumers' Capitalism* needs such directions because it is *unfair;* it is not *righteous.*

It is unfair, it is claimed, because it is too harsh. In such a system no man is supreme; in the final analysis, he must accept the responsibility for himself. Or, perhaps it may be argued that *Consumers' Capitalism* is not fair because prices aren't fair. (They are either too high, or too low.) The wage earner feels his wages are never high enough, and that his food costs are always too high. To the farmer, it seems the prices for which he sells his product are never high enough, and the cost of hired hands is invariably exorbitant. Or again, it is not fair because the more efficient, harder working individual comes off better than one who is less efficient and works less.

The charge that *Consumers' Capitalism* is unfair is leveled at managers, businessmen and entrepreneurs. It should be directed at the consumer, for if the system is not fair it is because of the consumer, who always hastens to buy the best for less. In the process, a chain of events is set in motion, which actualizes a natural reality wherein an individual is responsible for himself, where he cannot set prices at whim, and where the most efficient, most industrious workers earn the best wages.

In addition, it is charged that *Consumers' Capitalism* is not righteous. Evil profit leads men astray. Men should live according to some set of higher values. Whoever makes this statement then proceeds (without stopping for breath) to outline these higher values, whereupon it becomes apparent he is outlining his own particular values —which he would like to see accepted as the universal standard.

In actuality, *Consumers' Capitalism* allows each man to live within whatever economic sphere he chooses. The composite of these individual choices is responsible for the direction of the production/consumption cycle, and answers the basic economic questions. To the extent an individual better serves his fellow man, he profits more; to the extent he chooses not to do so, he is economically penalized. No one person, or group, is allowed to define the higher values for someone else within the economic realm.

A pseudo-intellectual may call for government support of the arts. It never occurs to him that in a free system of *Consumers' Capitalism*, if people want more cultural activity they will rush to art galleries and opera houses; and, by their freely-stated demand, cause more of these services to be created. That they do not, is conclusive evidence there are other things the consumers consider more important at present. When the pseudo-intellectual persists in his call for government-supported art, he is saying, in effect, that even though most people do not want more of it, he does; and further, that his own personal desires should be government-financed!

In the *Middle Way,* just as in *Bureaucratic Capitalism,* the password is planning. The difference is merely one of degree. In *Bureaucratic Capitalism* the ideal is to plan everything; in combining the two systems it is considered desirable only to plan some activities, leaving some areas to operate in freedom. The result is a method in which *Bureaucratic Capitalism* is overlaid upon a base of *Consumers' Capitalism.*

The result may be referred to as a directed, controlled, mixed, or planned economy; or depending upon the point of view, a hampered market or interventionism. The

right kind of bureaucratic tampering with *Consumers'
Capitalism* will then supposedly correct the faults of a
free market, with the emergent system a combination
designed to deliver the best of both.

Such a bastardized system cannot be precisely defined
because of the large number of variations possible in an
economy where *Bureaucratic Capitalism* and *Consumers'
Capitalism* co-exist. For example, such an economy may
consist of proportionately more *Bureaucratic Capitalism*
to less *Consumers' Capitalism,* or vice-versa.

The exact ratio varies from nation to nation and from
time to time; depending upon the values of those who
hold the reigns of power, and the efficacy of whatever
checks may be imposed upon their authority. Short of
full dictatorial control, any economy is a mixture of both
systems, where hindrances (excluding restraint of crimi-
nal activity) are placed upon the free expression of individual economic value choices.

Does It Work?

Any bridge for reaching a middle ground between
Consumers' Capitalism and *Bureaucratic Capitalism* must
be built upon the system of the former. We have already
seen the inherent impossibility of a complete system of
Bureaucratic Capitalism, where there is no market for a
guide. Those who would "improve" man's economic
organization in this manner start with a market system
and seek to "make it better," i.e., to reach other values
than those which an unhampered market system would

produce. This intervention is intended to make *Consumers' Capitalism* into something it would not otherwise become. The free market moves naturally in a certain direction, and will move in a different one only by application of force.

Economics is the study of those means men use to achieve their ends, but economics does not set ends, in and of itself. This being so, we can expect our examination of interventionism to reveal whether the government actually can achieve the ends it proclaims, through interference with the free market. The answer is yes, sometimes.

Occasionally, the government may reach a desired goal by applying force and limiting its citizens' freedom in the market. Theory and empirical evidence both indicate, however, that many times a government can fail to achieve its avowed objectives in the economic field by exerting force; frequently, effects exactly opposite from the proclaimed intentions result. (An explanation of interventionism will demonstrate how this occurs.)

So often do the results of government intervention differ from announced intentions that we must be led to two conclusions. The first might be that the Bureaucrats themselves do not understand economics and therefore take a superficial view; not realizing that the economic process is an interrelated one.

The second, more probable conclusion might be that the Bureaucrats really do know the effect of interventionism upon the economy, but for obvious reasons don't say so out loud. In some instances, where laws are passed which directly benefit a particular group at the expense of another, this would seem the logical explanation. In the following examination of interventionism, we shall assume (unless specifically mentioned otherwise) that the Bureaucrats are operating under the first assumption, and do not fully understand the process of economics.

In a study of governmental policy we need not be overly concerned with two methods the authorities may use to influence the economy. One method may be termed "political window dressing"—laws read onto the books which look good, and show the Bureaucrats to be nice fellows, worthy of confidence. (In actuality, the conditions under which these laws operate are such that the law makes no difference anyway.)

The other method, mentioned only in passing, is the direct attempt on the part of authorities to influence consumption. Any tampering with the economy will influence consumption one way or another—either in the short run, the long run, or both.

Thus, a campaign directed at the populace (by the government) against drinking alcoholic beverages, reading erotic books, or seeing pay TV in their own homes will directly affect consumption of these items in such a way that economic reasoning is not required to understand it. The economy simply shifts direction from these proscribed activities into others. A black market (or free market) may then arise in the forbidden commodities, depending upon consumer demand and the ability of the police force to maintain control. When a black market does come into being, the consumers must then pay the higher costs necessitated by the premium on illegal activity. The rationale used to explain these direct and limiting actions is that the Bureaucrats must protect the citizens, who are presumably too dull, stupid, lazy, or indifferent to know better; the implication being that the authorities do know better. This rationale also shows up in other, more subtle attempts to regulate the economy.

The Interventionist Fallacies

One of the most interesting conclusions reached by the interventionist is the naive belief that prosperity can somehow be created by simply passing a law, or issuing a decree. For example, a law setting a minimum wage will supposedly give everyone a minimum subsistence standard. But if this can be done by merely reading a statute on the books, why not make the minimum wage $25.00 per hour, and let everybody get rich?

The central fallacy from which this reasoning stems is the assumption that economic production is just simply there; that output is something which flows on and on, regardless of any tampering, obstacles, or hindrances placed in its path. The interventionist chooses not to see that production is the result of individual effort, or that a point can be reached where a sufficient number of obstacles will slow down or altogether stop such effort.

Shoes are not lying in the woods, waiting to be picked up by anyone who needs a pair; nor are they waiting there, ready-made, for the governmental authorities to distribute as they see fit. Someone must first make the shoes. Someone must buy the leather, thread, and other supplies, and put them together. This is true whether the shoes are made by hand or with the aid of computers and automated machinery. When finished, the shoemaker—not the government—has a pair of shoes.

The more difficult the government makes shoe production for the shoemaker, and the heavier he is taxed after the shoes are made, the less inclination he will have to produce shoes. Carried far enough, this process will cause production of shoes to be discontinued altogether.

A similar fallacy is involved in the interventionist doctrine of public ownership. "Let the government initiate the production (in certain important areas), and it will then not only be safe from crippling effects of government interference; but since it is also publicly owned, all will benefit."

Unfortunately, such public ownership is, at best, a sham. The crucial test of ownership is the ability of the owner to use his property, or transfer title to someone else, as he sees fit. It makes no difference that, by some far-fetched theory, each of us is a fractional owner of the U.S. Post Office system. We must nevertheless use its facilities according to the rules determined by the Bureaucrats, who operate the system. And try to sell your pro-rata share of the U.S. Post Office!

Still another fallacy of interventionism involves the human element. All governmental planning involving the use of force must lead eventually to graft, corruption, and inefficiency. Scandals of this sort are regularly uncovered throughout the civilized world. It is a natural, built-in accompaniment to bureaucratic intervention—because, even if all the public administrators were supermen in their fairness and discriminatory abilities, they must still involve themselves with such things as the granting of licenses, quotas, franchises, zoning requisitions, tax exemptions, etc. That such sanctions exist means that the privileges bestowed by these administrators are limited to receipt by a comparative few. Otherwise, there would be no need for issuing them.

The authorities have no way to determine who should receive the privileges, and who should not. They are charged with acting from a "higher sense of values," whereupon it again becomes a question of *whose* values. Certainly, not those of the general population (the consumers), for to act in their behalf would result in *Consumers' Capitalism*, with no attendant necessity for government intervention.

In real life, governments are composed of men, who, because they are human beings, are not omniscient. One of the most unfortunate phenomena of our time is that many voters forget their governments are made up of people; hence, government directions are the decisions of various men and are not the sole, absolute, unqualified source of righteous action.

Bribery and corruption inevitably enter into human dealings. Some Bureaucrats, being men, will take a fast buck when it is offered to them. If there is no alternative available, the citizenry is stuck. In a free market society an individual may choose not to deal with a suspect character—he can always go elsewhere. When the government reigns supreme within a given sphere, consumer choice is squeezed out. The growing bureaucratic agencies tend to become peopled with men owning wealth of undetermined origin. Administrative hirelings and influence-peddlers become important in our civilization, and young men graduating from school are told, "It's not what you know, but who you know."

Apologists for government intervention are always conceding (after any program has been in effect for a while) that "yes, the program does need to be cleaned up; yes, we do need to take some of the abuses out of it; but despite these flaws, the basic idea is still a good one." Someday the realization must come that it is impossible to clean up any interventionist program where ungod-like men are given god-like power.

A Worldwide System

Thus far, we have seen that the *Middle Way*, unlike the systems of *Consumers' Capitalism* and *Bureaucratic Capitalism*, is not a pure system, but a conglomerate of the two; and is practiced throughout the world. In each country it varies, according to the extent of the free market in use, and the amount of forcible, bureaucratic intervention.

We have stated how, in some ways (such as through direct prohibition of certain items), governments can steer the economy into pre-determined channels, though even this is made difficult by the existence of black (free) markets. By listing the interventionalist fallacies, which regard production as occurring automatically, consider public ownership to be universally beneficial, and assume administrators to be divine, we have shown many of the problems the intervention faces. Further, we have said that the results of such systems are frequently not in keeping with their proclamations.

In the following chapters, we shall examine some of the areas where intervention goes astray; beginning with theoretical considerations, and proceeding to a brief analysis of acute, present-day problems and their relation to intervention.

We shall use, for illustration, the economy of the United States. Historically, the United States has been one of the nations with the least amount of free market intervention (though never completely free); and as a result the necessary impetus was provided for turning a wilderness into the envy of the world, in less than two centuries. But the seeds of governments using force and coercion to interfere with private economic life have always been with us; and shortly before World War I, they began to sprout anew.

After the Great War, nations began massive economic intervention. Mussolini's Corporate State, the Communists in Russia, the Nationalist Socialist Workers (Nazi) Party in Germany, and the American New Deal were all examples of the worldwide tendency of governments seemingly dedicated to the single idea that an ever-increasing crops of Bureaucrats could solve all economic ills. Today the names have been changed but the idea, now mellowed and sanctified by tradition, remains basically the same.

The United States, nonetheless, remains one of the freer nations of the world; there is a lesser proportion of *Bureaucratic Capitalism* in relation to the amount of *Consumers' Capitalism* operative. "Freer", here, is a relative term. The government owns outright, or exerts the dominant influence on: streets and highways, letter delivery, schools, the banking system, printing of money, most agriculture, all forms of transportation, the wage structure, and individual industry groups (such as natural gas, electric power, water supply, fire-fighting, money-lending, radio and TV broadcasting, atomic energy development, and so on). Add to these the industries where government is the sole buyer, and we have a staggering list.

Any government, possessing not only police and army to give punch to its laws, but also such an awesome collection of economic power, must assuredly be able to have its desires responded to within the economy. The Bureaucrats' value choices, rather than those of the consumer, will come to be expressed in economic activity. We shall now proceed to see how this takes place, and what happens when it does.

Chapter 11

GOVERNMENT REVENUES

Public Finance

Governments don't earn money by exchanging goods and services on the market, as do individuals. Governments aren't organized for production, as is the entrepreneur; nor do they profit from efficiency They do not perform labor as a worker does, thereby receiving wages; they are not primarily in the business of leasing land or capital and collecting rents. They may do some of these things tangentially to governing, and collect money thereby, but the resulting funds are never an important source of revenue. Governments collect the money to operate chiefly through taxes.

Government may tax the citizenery outright; it may borrow money from individuals, and tax future genera-

tions to repay the loans; government may print paper
and call it money, or engage in a similar process with bank
credit (the maneuver known as inflation). Inflation, which
is a dilution of the monetary unit, is actually a levy on
every bank account, insurance policy, annuity or other
saving. It has been called "the cruelest tax of all".

Taxes always have a double-barreled effect on the economy. The economy is influenced according to when,
where, and how the government obtains the revenues; and
again influenced according to when, where, and how the
government spends the money thus obtained. We shall look
more closely at the citizenry half of the taxing process concerned with government spending in following chapters.
For the present, it is sufficient to note that the spending of
tax money by Bureaucrats, on behalf of government pro-
grams of redistribution within a mixed economy, invariably means money being spent in other ways than those
which the consumer would choose. When consumer-
citizens are given free choice in spending their own money,
a system of *Consumers' Capitalism* is operative; therefore,
it would be pointless to employ professional Bureaucrat-
spenders to spend money for projects or commodities
which the consumers would have purchased anyway.

With this understanding we arrive at the basic assumption and *raison d' etre* for taxes in a mixed economy. It
is this: "The citizens who earn the money are too
ignorant or cruel to know how to spend their own money;
therefore, certain sums must be taken from them by force

and coercion, and placed into the hands of the Bureaucrats —who are better qualified to spend such money."

The immediate effect of taxation is the setting up of two distinct classes of people among the population. Some become net taxpayers; some net tax receivers. Regardless of how much or how little an individual pays in taxes; regardless of the amount the individual receives, in the form of government services—when these are set off against each other on an individual level, a person either pays more to the government on balance, or receives more from it on balance. This creates a new problem, which does require Bureaucrats to be expert spenders. Who is to be allowed in which group?

In *Consumers' Capitalism*, wealth automatically flows to those who produce, so the entrepreneur, the land owner, the owner of capital, and the wage earner are all compensated according to the value the consumer places upon his contribution to the production/consumption cycle. In a mixed economy, producers have their production partially taken from them through taxes and placed in a "pool," which the Bureaucrats administer. Then, concern with the distribution or redistribution of wealth becomes unavoidable.

The taxation process is called "Public Finance," which carries the hopeful implication that the study of economics will reveal the proper redistribution of the producers' confiscated wealth. But it is a call to which economics cannot respond. The decision as to whom should be entitled to production, other than the producer, does not lie within the confines of economics. Economic analysis can deal only with the effect of taxes on the production/consumption cycle, and that effect is both clear and generally well known. If producers aren't allowed to own their production, they have less incentive to produce.

Given a situation where producers are allowed to keep less and less of their production—all other things being equal—the incentive to produce will slacken, with a subsequent decrease in production (relative to what it would otherwise have been). New machines and techniques in concurrent use may result in an actual physical increase in output; yet this increase is less than it would have been, were the government not engaging in redistribution schemes.

The division of the populace into two reciprocally suspicious groups of net taxpayers and net tax receivers gives insight into some political activity in general, and certain lobbying and pressuring tactics in particular. Many regard the currying of favor with the government (in order to be in the net tax receiver group) as preferable to being in the net taxpayer group. This situation also shows why the old saw, "Taxes don't make any difference; we are only taxing and paying ourselves" is complete fallacy. If an individual is in the net taxpayer group, he is being taxed to pay someone else, and it does make a difference—especially to him.

Outright Taxation

The effect of taxes is decrease of production, in two ways. Producers are discouraged from increasing output, and incentive for investment is lessened. When there is decrease in production there is less available for consumption, so consumption rates fall. Hence, taxes are ultimately paid for by a reduction in total consumption, as compared with what it could have been, in the absence of a tax.

This is the result, no matter what kinds of taxes (or combinations of taxes) are being levied. If taxes are applied to specific items or industries, these groups are penalized as costs are artificially raised; if taxes are applied to specific individuals, these people are discouraged from greater effort; if taxes are levied overall, the debilitating effect is spread, more or less, throughout the entire economy.

Quite naturaly, men and material will flow from areas of higher taxation to lower taxed areas, whenever they can. Consequently any tax which does not leave the market in the exact condition it was found will cause distortions as factors of production go elsewhere, to seek higher returns. A tax giving preferential treatment to natural resources or capital gains will induce additional factors into these lines which would not have gone there in the absence of a special tax advantage. This is one of the many subtle ways in which government interference levers the economy into channels it would not otherwise take.

Similarly, no one has yet discovered a way to tax *leisure;* its consumption is therefore tax-free. As taxes advance, and an individual sees substantial amounts of the fruits of his labor being taken from him he is more inclined to leisure rather than to additional production. In advanced economies, where the standard of living is considerably above subsistence level, this tendency will be especially strong.

Recognizing that taxation reduces incentive and thereby lowers consumption, economists have long searched for a neutral tax—one which could be imposed without causing a decline in production and investment. So far, such a tax has not been found, not is it likely to be. The fact that taxes must be collected by threat of force lends serious doubt to any possibility of neutrality in taxation. However, within the nature of various kinds of taxes is the inherent characteristic that some will be less distortive to the economy than others.

If the government taxes individual items or industries, the result is a diminished production of the taxed commodity. Upon the imposition of such a tax on automobiles, for example, the auto manufacturers do not necessarily raise prices by the amount of the tax, passing it on to the buyer (as is popularly assumed). If the market is free, automobiles are already selling for a price at which demand and supply are either in balance, or moving rapidly toward such a state. If, as a result of the tax levy, the auto makers raise the price of automobiles, they will find less demand than at lower prices and must thus cut back production. If they do not raise the price of their cars but absorb the tax themselves, then it is really the auto makers who are paying the tax.

In a competitive situation of high tax and low profits the less efficient producers begin to drop by the wayside as losses force them out of business. Remaining producers have very little incentive to expand production to make up for those who leave the field. In either case, production falls and capital, workers, and entrepreneurs are attracted to other ventures where greater returns are anticipated.

A graduated or progressive tax on income brings forth those effects most likely to discourage production and investment; the more industrious and productive a man, the more tax he must pay. In a free system, a producer of goods and services the consumer most desires receives the highest income. When a graduated income tax is imposed, it is precisely the individual who is deemed most valuable to the production/consumption cycle who becomes most discouraged from increasing his contribution to the economic process.

Also, to the extent which a graduated feature takes money away from the individual, money he would use for investment, it lowers investment; at the same time, reducing the return from investment and narrowing the actual difference between present and future goods (which further hinders investment).

When labor shortages occur within an advanced economy it is frequently the most highly skilled worker who is in short supply. Because such an individual is in demand he enjoys high wage rates. In the United States, we have been hearing for some time about a scarcity of doctors, dentists, scientists, engineers, and various technicians. Even if the market system were allowed to work normally, it would take some time to fill these vacancies because of the lengthy training periods necessary for such occupations. The graduated feature of the income tax gives little economic incentive to induce such specialists (particularly the most competent) to increase individual output. To do so would mean the using up of their leisure in order to purchase less return per unit of labor. It is understandable that many, under these conditions, are more interested in closing the office one afternoon each week, taking longer vacations, or retiring earlier.

Inheritance taxes lower saving and investment, by providing a stimulus for people to either earn less or spend more, rather than to engage in accumulation of wealth which will be confiscated by the state upon their deaths. Here again, the graduated feature exaggerates the tendency.

A general sales tax reduces investment, production and consumption—although, since it is diffused over the widest possible base, its impact is not immediately apparent. The effect can best be seen when viewed in its entirety, for which the following illustration may be of help:

On Day 1 at :01 minutes, the government begins a general sales tax on everything sold. By 12 o'clock midnight, it has collected one million dollars in taxes. Where did this one million dollars come from? Clearly it came from the taxpayer, and represents money which he now cannot use for his individual consumption or investment.

Since the effect of taxes is decrease of production, taxes can reach a point at which they become self-defeating. A particular tax can be useful for reaping revenue only within certain limits. When the tax is continually raised, it reaches the point where those paying it will discover they are better off not engaging in the endeavor being taxed, and will act accordingly.

Chief Justice Marshall said, "The power to tax is the power to destroy." Individual men have always sensed this (even when their governments have not), and taxes, throughout history, have been a touchy subject. Hence, we see contemporary government—whenever it wishes to spend more money—busily searching for "new sources of revenue," i.e., places where taxes can be increased with the least resistance from the citizenry.

Considering the economy as a whole, the level of taxation is of more importance than the specific kind of tax levied. All taxes discourage production, but there is vast difference in the amount of discouragement caused by a 1% tax, and that caused by a 50% tax. Economics does not have a precision instrument for conducting such a measurement, but the observations made thus far would lead us to believe that, within the context of today's advanced economies, a 1% or 2% overall tax would be practically negligible in its economic effect.

As taxes go higher, production diminishes, until it is eventually destroyed altogether. Because of this fact, the finest hope of the planners who would mix their *Bureaucratic Capitalism* in the soil of *Consumers' Capitalism* is forever doomed. High taxes and *Consumers' Capitalism* are incompatible. The thought itself is a contradiction. Consumers cannot spend money of their free choice, while at the same time Bureaucrats are taking away sizable chunks of it.

The Magic of Borrowing

In addition to taxation, the government may borrow money to raise revenue. It may borrow from the individual citizen, and give him its I.O.U's, such as Series "E" Savings Bonds (or Defense Bonds, or War Bonds, depending upon the current political situation). The government enjoys special status as a borrower, since the redemption of its obligations does not rest upon its ability to satisfy a shifting demand in the market place, but rather, on its control of police and army to enfore tax collections. Therefore, its bonds are regarded as being the least risky of investments, and it has no trouble raising funds in the money market.

When the government uses this method of finance, it sops up private cash which would have otherwise gone into investment; the net result is a shift from private investment activities—which the consumer wants—to bureau-

cratic spending. At a future time, the individual lender
becomes due for repayment and when the government
collects taxes to repay previous borrowing, it once again
diverts spending from what the consumer wants. In the
meantime, it must pay interest on the debt; and this interest is also furnished by the taxpayer.

In essence, government borrowing of cash from its
citizens is a type of "fly now, pay later" plan. Father can
have his spree, letting the Bureaucrats spend all kinds of
money; but years later—usually when the purchased goods
are no more than memories in a history book—his son
must pick up the check.

"The government debt doesn't matter, because we owe
it to ourselves," is a fallacy—in just the way the same idea,
as it applies to taxes, is a fallacy. Jones paid good money
for his government bonds, counting them as assets; it
would be impossible to convince him his bonds could, in
fairness, be declared worthless.

Smith, who owns no bonds, will not agree that the debt
doesn't matter either; for at tax time, as he shells out to
buy back Jones' maturing obligations, he will be aware of
the government debt. The country is made up of Joneses
and Smiths. The distortive effect of taxing one to pay the
other does matter.

Governments may not only borrow from the individual;
they may also borrow from banks. The latter course involves a special aspect of borrowing which is usually more
important than that of individual lending. If the govern-

ment should spend 100 billion in the current fiscal year, and should take in 95 billion in taxes and other collections, it would have to find the additional 5 billion elsewhere.

There are several difficulties involved in seeking money through loans from individuals—not the least of which is that if the government were to do so on the scale required by contemporary deficit financing, large amounts of private investment would be drained from the economy.

Another method for obtaining money needed, in our example, might be by cranking up the printing presses, and converting so many tons of paper into 5 billion dollars face-value of paper certificates called money. The trouble with this latter method is that it is too obvious. If people observe their government openly running new paper certificates they will—as Gresham's law states—try to avoid the certificates, or seek to dispose of them as soon as possible.

This extreme has been known to happen in countries where the government blatantly resorted to the printing press for resolving its payments problems—as witness the situation in Germany after World War I. Under these conditions, paper money becomes practically worthless; a sack of "money" will not buy a sack of potatoes.

The government may cover its deficits by borrowing from banks, which, under present conditions, is tantamount to printing new paper money. The distinction is that the process is so devious and complicated most people are unaware it is actually happening. Also, the process is kept within some kind of bounds so it will not reach the runaway stage.

The close tie between money and economic activity has been stressed throughout the previous pages. If governments want to influence the economy they begin by exercising some control over money. There has been an almost universal movement in this direction by all the governments in the world. Generally, such steps have been first, setting up a central banking system, in order to call the tune for all banks; next allowing only the central bank, or the treasury, to print money certificates. The rights of citizens to use gold is subsequently curtailed, and the government's paper certificates are made irredeemable in gold to its citizens, and declared to be legal tender.

The government may issue paper money, which is either backed partially, or not at all, with gold. Once this has been accomplished, the machinery is available which allows the government to legally make paper money out of thin air, so to speak. It may use this process in conjunction with deficit financing (when it borrows from banks), creating bank deposits instead of paper certificates.

Bank deposits are a money substitute, like paper currency, and are circulated as money. Later, the government may, if necessary, print paper currency in exchange for these bank deposits.

To illustrate this process, let us say the government needs fifty million dollars. It goes to the banks to borrow the money, giving the banks a governmental note (or bond) for the loan. The banks do not pay for the notes in cash, but rather, by crediting the government's checking account. The banks make entries in their ledgers, which show that the government has fifty million more on deposit; moreover, this fifty million of new demand deposits is backed up by a new bank asset of fifty million in government notes. Fifty millions of new money has been manufactured—just like that!

Further, the banks engage in fractional reserve banking. This means they do not keep a dollar in cash on hand for every dollar of deposit, despite the fact that deposits are redeemable on demand. Instead, they make loans on the theory that not every depositor will demand his money at the same time. Hence, an increase in the bank's assets will allow making of loans in amounts many times that of the increase.

For example, if the bank should be maintaining 10% in reserves against customer requests for cash, a new $1.00 asset will allow almost $10.00 to be made in loans. $10.00 is created in new demand deposits, while a 10% reserve (or $1.00) is still being held against the new deposits. The government, by tying up the banking system into a neat and tidy network— under the guise of public protection —makes fractional reserve banking easier, and builds a mechanism whereby its own monetary expansion or contraction activities may be multiplied many-fold. The bureaucratic control over the banks and the money supply is exercised through a multitude of banking laws; by buying and selling government obligations on the open market; and through the power of the Federal Reserve to set reserve requirements and discount rates. Using these means the authorities manage the money supply to whatever extent they consider appropriate.

The idea of a government creating money out of thin air to pay some of its bills may seem, at first glance, to be a wonderful, painless way to get something for nothing. But in economics there is no such thing as "something for nothing." Sooner or later, everything must be paid for by someone, somewhere. In fact, the real cost of this credit process is so expensive and tragic we shall deal with it later, in a separate section concerning inflation.

Chapter 12

INFLUENCING PRODUCTION

Restriction and Encouragement

Bureaucrats sometimes act to directly encourage production; sometimes they act to restrict it. There is no economic consistency in these actions, so it is impossible to tell if governments are for, or against, greater production. The answer depends on the data of each separate case, and is determined by the "higher values" the Bureaucrats are pursuing. A study of the nature of man's productive-consumptive activities reveals that government encouragement and government restriction of production amounts to the same thing. This is so because the factors of land, labor, and capital are limited; and more of the factors at use in one place means there are fewer available for use in another. Conversely, discouraging economic

170

factors in one area causes them to flow elsewhere.

For example, the Bureaucrats may encourage the production of housing by any of several methods, such as the granting of special tax advantages to owners of housing or by the insuring of loans; but to whatever extent housing is successfully increased, men and material are attracted to housing construction rather than other ventures, leaving behind them production declines. If discouragement of housing construction should be sought by means of a law denying adequate rental return, fewer men and material will be engaged in this creative activity.

Thus, while it may be true that the Bureaucrats can achieve encouragement or restriction within a specific endeavor, because of the interrelated characteristic of economic activity this achievement will have an opposite effect (albeit, not so obvious) elsewhere in the economy. Government attempts to encourage housing can cause contruction of housing, giving the outward appearance of economic gain; but not considered are those things which might have been created, had the time, effort, and material not been expended for additional housing. This is the initial cost of the government intervention. Further cost ensues, due to the readjustment and waste involved as the economy shifts from what the consumer wants to what the Bureaucrats want.

Still another cost is the added variable with which the entrepreneur must contend as he strives to anticipate future market conditions; for not only must tomorrow's possibilities be consideed as they might exist in a free economy, but also any distortion caused by whatever route bureaucratic action may take.

An illustration of the two-sided effect of bureaucratic restriction and encouragement of production is provided by reviewing the relationship of government and taxation. Government taxes its citizens, thereby restricting their spending, which lessens production in those areas where the citizens would have spent their money, had it not been taxed away from them. Then the Bureaucrats spend the money they collect, thereby encouraging production in the areas they want to favor.

In times past, bureaucratic spending of confiscated tax money has been regarded as having certain magic properties—a phenomenon better known as the "multiplier" effect. Thus, when the government spends money, it creates jobs; and these job-holders spend, creating more jobs; and so on, in a wonderful cycle of prosperity. The government may use some of its tax money to build beautiful bridges, buildings, and museums; it is easy for the public to see these magnificent structures, and to reason that if it were not for taxation such edifices would not exist. What is missing from such reasoning (because it cannot be seen, but must be envisioned to be understood), is the ability to imagine those things which could have been created from sources of private spending and production with the resources which have been used in these government projects.

If the government takes less in taxes, thereby leaving more in the hands of the consumers, the spending will remain the same. The difference is that Jones will be spending his own dollars, instead of handing them over to Bureaucrat *A*, who will spend them for him; and the economy will then move along different lines. Were this actually the case, we would see less economic activity devoted to an accelerated moon race for purposes of "national prestige," or less energy expended to build a seaport in Oklahoma; instead, there would be more to spend for cars, television, homes, clothes, travel, education, health service, savings—whatever commodities people most desire. All such desired goods come into being in response to increased consumer demand.

Limiting Production

Every handicap to production limits or curtails output. It is self-evident that restriction diminishes production, which means lower consumption. Therefore, when government undertakes to restrict production, either the "higher values" achieved must be deemed worth the price of decreased output, or else the officials aren't aware of the economic cost involved.

Two groups are immediate losers in all attempts to restrict production: the producers, who cannot produce as much as the market calls for; and the consumers, who cannot have as much of the item as they would like to have. Three groups are possible beneficiaries of restriction: other producers, who have a similar product which may be substituted for the proscribed commodity; illegal operators, who will bootleg the restricted product; and the Bureaucrats, who create an additional bureaucracy to oversee the curtailing of production. In every case, restriction must be attached to a functioning productive process already in operation, and can only result in slowing it down.

Other than through direct and indirect taxation, the authorities have countless ways available to restrict production such as the imposition of tariffs, which lessen the amounts of certain kinds of foreign-made goods on the market; quotas of all kinds—ranging from limiting the output of Texas oil wells, to how much cotton may be planted; licenses and franchises—which give permission to some for performing economic services, and exclude all others; specific restrictive laws, from Anti-Trust decrees (to prevent business from extending their services, in fields where they are most efficient) to law forbidding the sale of liquor to Indians. Government ownership is yet another means to restrict production—where resources are withheld from development by bureaucratic fiat.

Government ownership of natural resources, and the withdrawing of these resources from private development by the entrepreneur, is usually done under the guise of "conservation." In a previous section the myth of stealing from future generations has already been exploded. To this, should now be added the observable fact that such conservation by governing bodies is, in practice, the opposite of what it is supposed to be. If the resources are made available to private owners the pressure of the market will call upon each owner to utilize the resources to the best interest of the consumer; in this way, returning to the owner the highest profit.

In order to attain the highest profit, each owner must make the best possible use of his property. Under private ownership the impetus is toward thrift, care, and best usage of property by the owner, because the market penalizes waste—as it penalizes every other failure to economize.

In the instance of government (or public) ownership, the resource is, for practical purposes, ownerless except for periods of direction by Bureaucrats whose tenure is unsure; there is no economic incentive to make best use of the resource for as long as possible.

Assets will be wasted by not being used, wasted by being used in ways which the consumer would not support voluntarily, or wasted by abuse. Almost anyone will throw out a beer can in a public park. Practically no one will do so in his own front yard. This is the essential economic difference between public and private property.

The question of tariffs is one area which has been examined so thoroughly by economists that the cost of this kind of restriction is widely understood. The tariff problem is now mainly a political one. Through the use of tariffs the importation of foreign goods is hindered, so that the consumer is forced to purchase higher-priced domestic goods. This helps certain domestic producers, at the expense of the consumer.

The specialization of labor has resulted in enormous increases in overall production on an individual, local, and national level; and it stands to reason such specialization could have the same effect at an international level. In a free world market it is the tendency for each nation to specialize in producing those things for which it is best equipped, and to swap with other countries doing the same. All are thereby enriched by the increase in productivity.

This principle will be well recognized in the growing of citrus fruit, or mining ore. The comparative advantages of raising oranges in a mild climate, or mining iron where it is readily accessible, is obvious. What is not so obvious (though equally true) is that each nation, as a result of its historical, geographical, sociological, and economic development, enjoys comparative advantages over other nations in the production of many and various native items. Free trade allows each nation to do whatever it is best able to do, so all nations will benefit.

International trade is based upon swapping goods among nations. If, for the moment, we disregard money, we can see that if Andorra wants to send wool to Zanzibar in return for spices, it can do so only to the extent which Zanzibar is willing to take wool in trade. This is a way of saying imports must be paid for by exports.

The use of money greatly facilitates international trade —just as (for the same reason) a medium of exchange facilitates any trading activity. With the use of money merchants are no longer bound to cumbersome barter, and Andorra may obtain spices without swapping wool directly to Zanzibar. It may, instead, sell its wool elsewhere for money, and with the proceeds buy spices from Zanzibar.

Nonetheless, the use of money does not change the basic nature of international trade—*imports must still be paid for by exports.* (The terms imports and exports include not only physical commodities, but such intangibles as banking or shipping services, tourism, etc.)

There is one exception to the rule that imports must be paid for by exports, and that is when a nation gives away its products, or has products given to it. (Historically, this has occurred in recognizable proportion only once: in the case of U.S. foreign aid.)

When imports are curtailed, a drop in exports will follow. Potential foreign buyers, cut off from selling in the domestic market, have no way of obtaining funds with which to purchase in the domestic market. Thus, the imposition of tariffs not only acts as a tax on the consumer, who cannot then buy foreign goods as cheaply, but simultaneously lessens total business activity in the export industries.

One persistent argument for tariffs in the United States is the emotion-laden statement that if there were no tariff protection our domestic markets would be flooded with imports made by cheap foreign labor; with a consequent loss of American jobs. Free trade allows nations to specialize in that which each does best; with the advent of free trade we would no doubt see cheap labor products increasingly imported into this country. A related drop in employment within competing domestic industries would occur. But the story does not end there. Foreign nations, having sold more goods here, would have more dollars which must be spent here, and would become better customers for more of our own goods. As they bought more from the export industries business would pick up and employment increase in those areas.

America has a comparative advantage in the production of goods requiring technical know-how, capital investment, and mass production; and these are items for which there is an unfilled, worldwide demand. United States producers cannot compete as successfully on the world market in items where unskilled labor is a major cost component—say, for example, artificial plastic flowers, or inexpensive clothing. Nations having an abundance of unskilled labor can produce these types of goods more cheaply. But there is no reason for American manufacturers to compete on this level. There are sufficient areas remaining where the U.S. can engage in the world market advantageously; for only a small number of nations manufacture motor cars, few make airplanes, and fewer still are capable of making electronic computer systems—at least, not on a competitive basis.

Because of the comparative advantage the U.S. enjoys in such areas of production, these industries pay higher wages than others. Hence, in spite of the belief that tariffs protect Americans from cheap, foreign labor, tariffs (in the long run) inhibit the shift of workers into higher-paying jobs.

The most popular bureaucratic restrictions are in the field of labor. Here, the government may either act directly, or may lend its power to labor unions, so that they may enforce their edicts by coercion. Restrictions in this economic area are popular because many believe that a law to forbid child labor, shorten the work week, or limit the numbers of bricks a bricklayer may lay is a great gain for everyone who works.

Restricting production can never result in overall economic gain; rather, it must be paid for by decreased output. If, on an individual level, some receive more as a result of restriction, such individual gain must be paid for by individual loss somewhere else. In the case of the bricklayer, he receives a gain in that he has to lay fewer bricks per day; and when this is tied to a provision requiring the same pay as before, he is ahead since he does less work for the same pay.

To whatever extent the bricklayer is ahead, however, the consumer is immediately behind. Buildings of brick now cost more, and through the market process this cost will find expression either in higher prices for homes and buildings, higher rent for apartments and hotel rooms, etc.—or fewer will be built—or both. The bricklayer's gain becomes a hidden tax on the entire community.

Laws to shorten the work week have the same effect,

whether the laws prohibit work beyond a certain point or raise the price of such work (by requiring time-and-a-half pay, for example). Output is either curtailed or made more expensive. Because it is more expensive the product will find less acceptance in the market and less will be produced than otherwise.

The present shortened work week enjoyed in the western world is not the result of government laws or union demands. It is the result of ever-increasing production within the advanced nations, which has allowed workers (as well as everyone else) to provide for their material needs at the cost of less and less human effort. Machines invented, created, and directed by human ingenuity now do what men once had to do, laboriously, in order to survive. A law for an obligatory forty-hour work week in the eighteenth century, could it have been enforced, would have condemned millions to die from lack of sustenance— as would a similar law today in Asia, or Africa.

The short work week presently enjoyed by the population of the U.S. has not been bestowed through the generous grace of the government or unions. Rather, it has been the marvelous productive capacity of our economic system, running in high gear, which has made more material benefits and more leisure available at the same time. Individual employers cannot command their employees to work long hours at low pay, because the employees can earn sufficient wages (in shorter hours) elsewhere. It is capital accumulation which has raised the marginal utility of labor to its present height.

The same is true of those classic emotional complaints which accuse the market system of fostering child labor and sweatshops. It was not evil employers who forced people to work under miserable conditions. The workers came of their own accord because, however terrible the circumstances, at that time and place it was their only means of survival; and was far better than the starvation which faced their forefathers. Neither governments or unions can claim the credit for changing these conditions; such was not within their power.

Increasing output per worker has offered men the opportunity of working shorter hours in more pleasant surroundings, without requiring their children to work in order to help feed the family. These benefits are provided by the present, advanced state of production.

Unfortunate as it may be, the rude fact is that if restrictions against child labor and sweatshops were applied today in China or India a large part of their populations would be sentenced to death.

Encouragement

"Government encouragement of production" is but another name for government restriction of production! Since economic resources are scarce, if production is artificially encouraged in one area it must decrease somewhere else.

When we discussed tariffs under the category, *Restriction,* we talked about the aspect of tariffs which restricts the availability of foreign-made goods in the domestic market. We could just as easily classify tariffs under *Encouragement,* where, by making foreign goods more expensive, the Bureaucrats try to encourage domestic production. Hence, restriction and encouragement are part and parcel of the same phenomenon and must always be understood as such. However, since some bureaucratic measures have been labeled as official encouragement for so long, these traditional devices will be discussed separately.

Currently, much attention is being directed to the category of economic growth. Growth means an increase in total production, as measured from an arbitrarily chosen base. This increase is unanimously considered desirable by Bureaucrats everywhere, who seek to encourage the nation's economic growth.

Once again, the desire is to influence economic action along a path it would not otherwise take—and once again, individual men wish to make their own value choices, without being forced into the choices made by Bureaucrats. Necessarily, a clash occurs. As a practical matter, economic growth comes about through increased savings and investment; therefore, bureaucratic attempts to encourage growth will be aimed at developing such increases.

In a free market, savings and investment will be accumulated as millions of consumers make individual decisions regarding which portion of income to spend, and which to save. Each individual will grow financially to whatever extent he saves; anyone not wanting to grow in this way does not save—spending all his income, instead, on current consumption. The aggregate of these individual savings determine the amount of savings available, and how much the total investment and economic growth will be. Simultaneously, the consumer, by his spending, is showing in which areas this growth should take place.

When the government enters the picture, Bureaucrats habitually pick an arbitrary percentage figure for the nation's economic growth, and proceed to plan for this figure. But how can people be made to save more, when they do not want to? All answers lend to one conclusion, which is, ostensibly, taking the people's money in taxes and having the government *invest* it.

How does the government then invest it? Clearly not by building factories, stores, and the like, for there are enough of those already (as shown by the disinclination of people to save more money for the purpose of such additional construction); if the Bureaucrats do invest in this way some production facilities will operate at a loss because of insufficient demand—with resulting waste, and no increase in growth.

How about dams, roads, parks, government office buildings, and public monuments? Yes, the Bureaucrats can invest in these; thereby achieving a kind of national growth which will show itself in statistics.

Confiscating money from people in order to build things they want far less than the privilege of spending their own money can hardly be called national *growth*.

Economics is based upon the concept of individual, acting man. It is a mistake—a game with words—to label as *economic growth* the increased production of goods which people least desire, rather than of those they want most.

The king of such encouragement methods (in use since antiquity) is the *subsidy*. With this tool the authorities can directly encourage a pet group, while calling on all others to pay the cost of its favoritism. Subsidies run the gamut from the easily visible, such as tax exemptions and overpayment for carrying mail; to the more subtle, such as the giving of foreign aid.

Foreign aid was undoubtedly not initiated as a domestic subsidy; and economics does not pass judgement or whether foreign aid as help to other nations is good or bad. Economics delineates the effect of action within the economic sphere, and here it must point out the dollars given to other countries eventually return to the United States to be spent. When they do, American industries receive orders paid for by a tax on the citizenry. The taxpayers are subsidizing additional business for American companies even though foreigners receive the goods.

The most grandiose of all subsidies is the American agriculture subsidy; by looking at it we can see an example of government interference which has reached the absurd position at which all intervention must eventually arrive, if economic logic may be trusted. The rulers encourage production of specified farm commodities by setting an artificial price (higher than the world market price), and, through loans, buy the output at these prices. Farmers, seeking the higher prices, increase their crops to the point that the encouragement is a resounding success. Across the nation, storage bins overflow with the manipulated commodities. The authorities are faced with a new difficulty: there is so much of the encouraged products on hand they cannot be disposed of.

The Bureaucrats next resort to restriction, allowing only certain farmers to plant a given amount of the encouraged item. Farmers, spurred on by high prices (though now limited in productive acreage), increase production per acre, by capital expenditures.

Now the government begins a soil bank plan. Farmers are paid not to grow the encouraged commodity. Meanwhile, the surplus pile grows ever higher.

The last resort is payment of another subsidy to users of the encouraged commodity, in order to unload some of the surplus. This action is hastened, as when the voter realizes that foreign manufacturers can buy American cotton cheaper on the world maket than American manufacturers are allowed to buy it at home; and moreover, that foreign firms process this cotton into finished goods which compete with American-made goods.

The result of bureaucratic encouragement is clear. The "farm problem," as the politicians like to call it, is government-created. In freer areas of the economy we can find no parallel—there is no "automobile problem," or "shoe problem."

Yet, as pitiful and desperate as it seems, we have looked at only half of the story. The worst part is that the citizen must forego consumption of the things he wants, in order to pay the taxes to create the surplus. Had he been allowed to keep his money, and spend it in the manner he wished, countless industries would have been boosted by the added spending; jobs and prosperity in these lines would be much greater. Instead, human effort is directed into producing mammoth piles of commodities which become an end unto themselves; neither contributing further to production, nor benefiting anyone. They are the Twentieth Century pyramids.

Chapter 13

PLAYING WITH PRICES

Economic Reality and the Fix

Bureaucrats or influential groups who have access to the government's instruments of coercion often decide that certain prices would be desirable in the national economy. It is decided, for example, that everyone *should* have a nice apartment at a low rental, or that every worker is *entitled* to a minimum wage; that barbers *should* receive a minimum price for haircuts, or that to charge *too much* interest is mean and unfair. Having arrived at these great aims, the Rulers issue an edict setting the price of the commodity where they think it ought to be.

How easy it appears to be: "If cheap housing is needed, pass a law saying rents can't be raised; if workers want to earn more, pass the law setting a higher wage rate.

Eternal glory to our Law-Givers; everything we want can be ours by legislative fiat!"

Unfortunately, this kind of utopia is impossible to be had. If new legislation is all that is necessary, why not cut prices in half, so everyone can buy more? When economic thinking is applied to any attempt to *fix* a free market, we can see why these schemes prove unworkable.

In *Consumers' Capitalism* the market processes are interrelated; its parts are impossible to separate and be acted upon, singly. There is a systematic connection between cause and effect in social exchange. Things don't just happen at random. There is an interconnectedness of activity among individuals acting in the material sphere, and the science of economics is the understanding of these related phenomena. It is in this sense that we speak of economic laws—meaning the invariable actions and effects of those actions, among human beings engaged in social exchange. To be successful in analyzing economic problems we must realize the limitations which these laws place on human activity.

The prices of countless items used in modern life are not set by accident or some fortuitous circumstance. Rather, they are set by the constant interplay of supply and demand, acting within the context of available factors of production. Rental prices for housing, for example, are set by the interaction of those consumers desiring housing, and entrepreneurs providing housing. The idea that rents should be set at a level other than that upon which these groups have agreed is silly and absurd. When some group (or person) attempts to set the price it considers proper, contrary to the free market, this indicates the desire of such a group to become omnipotent, to be above the market, to overrule the free choice of other men.

The absolute interrelatedness of economic activity is such that the artificial distortions resulting from attempts to *fix* the market will become part of the market itself. The government planner cannot pick out a special item for favor or disfavor, without distubing the overall economy.

Setting Prices Too Low and Too High

In order to be able to judge the level of a particular price, there must be some standard to measure it against. *Too high* and *too low* are relative terms, making sense only if compared to something else which gives them proportion. The market price is the standard upon which those who seek to administer prices base their estimation. Some individual or group might decide that such-and-such a market price (freely arrived at by constant exchange in an atmosphere where no force or coercion is present) is wrong, and that the price should be set at a different level. (How this special knowledge has been arrived at is never divulged.)

Suppose some group should decide it would be nice if automobiles sold for $1,000. "A One-Grand Car" is a potent political slogan, so it elects its candidates to office, and passes into law a ceiling price on cars of $1,000. But after the law is passed unforeseen things begin to happen.

Finding that cars cannot profitably be manufactured to sell for $1,000, the automobile producers stop production. Some might continue for awhile, in the hope of better days ahead, but because each car is being sold at a loss these operations cannot continue indefinitely; when the money is gone, the manufacturing of automobiles will cease.

Compared with the ideal—a wonderful land, wherein everyone may easily afford a $1,000 car—reality is harsh indeed. Cars become scarce, because most of the manufacturers have been driven out of business by the low selling prices. At the same time, demand for these cheaper autos has soared. The inevitable result of fixing prices at the wrong level (lower than market price) occurs: the item begins to disappear from the market. The lower the fixed price, in comparison to market price, the more producers become marginal and fall by the wayside. The Bureaucrats must resort to some form of rationing to distribute the dwindling supply among increased consumer demand.

Because rationing is never popular, the Bureaucrats (having created the problem in the first place) seek a way out. As a solution an old favorite is called upon: the subsidy. If the auto factories cannot make enough cars to sell at $1,000—a telling example which "proves" private enterprise must have failed—the government must step in and subsidize the auto manufacturers, so they can produce enough cars.

It may appear that the example of "A One-Grand Car" is rather fanciful, and could not really happen; at least, not with automobiles. But suppose we change our example to the realm of housing; and to the results of ceilings on apartment rentals. On the basis of these same principles, we can visualize the beginning of a housing shortage. We can further envision the government moving to alleviate this shortage, by various subsidies such as guaranteed mortgage loans, urban renewal, slum clearance, and public housing. Is it fanciful to imagine *this* could happen?

Usually in setting prices the government does not begin by arbitrarily lowering an existing price; rather, it arbitrarily fixes the existing price as a "ceiling," beyond which the price may not rise.

The essence of economic activity, however, is "change." As time goes on, entirely different conditions may arise, which call for an alteration in prices. If the called-for change (by a free economy) is upward, which the Rulers have forbidden, artificial scarcity will occur—just as when the government fixed the price of cars at $1,000. To prevent such scarcity, it is necessary to "freeze" all prices —not only the price of the item in question, but the price of each component in the item, each of the component's components, and so on down the line, in an impossibly complex series. A "freeze" is lack of change. It is stagnation.

By setting prices too low in comparison with the market price, shortages are created. Conversely, if prices are set too high, the opposite happens and surpluses appear. There are more sellers wanting to sell at the abnormally high prices, than there are buyers wanting to buy . (We have already discussed the classic example of this law: the setting of high prices for farm commodities.)

Fixing a Crucial Price

Bureaucratic price-fixing of individual items has distortive consequences which, after directly affecting the price-fixed item, radiate out in diminishing degrees of influence to other points in the economy. But there is one price so basic to a modern economy that its manipulation immediately affects a host of other prices, and a major portion of economic activity. That price is interest—the price of a loan.

In terms of interventionists' economics, the traditional view has been that money should be cheap; interest, low; and borrowers favored over lenders. It is difficult to find an example in economic history of a consistent bureaucratic program aimed at maintaining high interest rates. Laws against high interest charges are legion. Since the dawn of antiquity Creditors have been pictured as rich, greedy money-lenders, living off the life-juices of innocent helpless debtors. There is no antonym in the English language for usury.

However true this view of borrowers and lenders might have been at one time, it is not the case at present. Today, the positions tend to be reversed. Millions of working men and women save, through such devices as insurance policies, bank accounts, pension plans, savings accounts, credit unions, stock purchases, government bonds, union funds, etc. The institutions involved loan out money; thus people of ordinary means are the creditors in today's world. Corporations and businessmen, popularly regarded as The Rich, are the active seekers of credit. The larger or richer they are, the more they can and will borrow. They are today's debtors.

Cheap money is erroneously regarded as the high road to prosperity. Individual Jones, or Entrepreneur Smith sees that if he can freely borrow at low interest he can afford to borrow and spend more; and these additional purchases will create more jobs and prosperity. Looking at it from such an individual point of view he is likely to lose sight of the fact that one man's borrowing is another man's lending (momentarily disregarding the creation of new money); therefore, he borrows and spends what someone else had, but did not spend, in order to make the loan.

Bureaucrats themselves may wish to keep the interest rate low. After a number of years of deficit financing the national debt may become exorbitant; and the interest payments involved in carrying the debt may become a sizable burden. These interest payments must come from the taxpayers, and a lower interest rate will mean less tax money diverted to payment of interest on the national debt. This desire, combined with the ideas that borrowers should be favored over lenders, and that low-cost loans create prosperity, fuse to form a seemingly irresistible siren's call. The authorities move toward making loans cheap, by lowering interest.

The interest rate is determined by the demand for funds, set against the supply available for lending. Two ways in which to lower interest rates are open to the Bureaucrats. One alternative is to act to hinder, or weaken, demand; but this would result in less borrowing—thereby defeating the original purpose. The other alternative is to increase the supply of money. We have outlined how the state, through control of the central banking system and its influence on the nation's banks, has available certain methods to increase bank credit money (and later, where necessary, to issue paper money in exchange for bank credit).

When the authorities want to lower interest rates they indulge in the process of manufacturing new money; making it available on the lending market where the increased supply acts to reduce the interest rate. Hence, the by-product of keeping interest rates low is the creation of more money, in the form of bank credit and paper dollars. The entire economic structure is built around exchanges based upon money prices, so that when additional money comse into existence it will affect all prices; causing repercussions in every nook and cranny throughout the economy.

Bureaucrats As Businessmen

When the government operates a business in an area

which could be served by private enterprise, it must fix prices directly. In such instances, prices are usually set by administrative decree or politics simply because there is no other way to determine them.

There is one rigid requirement for private individuals and firms who wish to remain in business: they must make a profit. Every sector of private industry withdraws economic resources from loss uses, and puts them into profitable operations. The profit test tells each business (on an individual level) if it should continue in business; and, on the level of the overall economy, the profit test tells whether or not the business is satisfying the consumer with its present use of resources. Those entrepreneurs who do not earn a profit, fail; and the economic factors which would have been used are released for re-allocation into processes where they will fill more urgent needs.

Governments, by the nature of their coercive powers, are not subject to this rule of the free market. When Bureaucrats decide they want to be in business they confiscate money (in the form of taxes) and set up shop. They do not have to be concerned with whether or not they make a profit; if they have losses they merely confiscate additional money to cover the shortages.

Because of this propensity, bureaucratically operated enterprises are not responsive to market direction, and can continue almost indefinitely to engage in allocations of economic resources which are not what the consumer wants. For the same reason, they can charge any price they choose for their product.

Sometimes, the government may operate its business as a monopoly by not allowing others to participate legally in the field. Other times it can achieve the same effect, or nearly so, by merely entering a particular line of endeavor. Its special advantages of having unlimited funds at its disposal or extra-ordinary borrowing power, of being exempt from taxes or any cost considerations, and not being concerned with making a profit and being able to set any price it likes (including giving away its product) will sooner or later put out or scare out most private competitors.

Together with exemption from normal demands of the market comes a tendency toward inefficiency. Because they need not especially concern themselves with operating costs, nor worry about being forced out of business by competition or shifting consumer demand, bureaucratic managers have little incentive to strive for efficacy. What little incentive there might be (supposedly built in by efficiency experts), is further undercut by political considerations which are, after all, of uppermost priority in government-operated enterprises. Thus, government in business not only wastes economic resources by diverting scarce factors into things the consumer wants least, but it does even this in an inefficient and costly manner.

There are four main arguments advanced by those who want government to be active in business:

1. *Government has always been involved in certain*

kinds of business, such as the Post Office.

This hardly needs to be commented upon. It is insufficient justification for any action to say that habit makes right.

2. *Government must do those things that private enterprise can't do.*

The critical point in examination of this proposition is the question, "What is government? And what constitutes private enterprise?" In this context, Government means a group of people assembled to perform certain functions; while private enterprise is also defined as a group of people assembled to perform certain functions. Translated into economic terms, this statement will now read: "People assembled in Group *A* must do those things which people assembled in Group *B* can not do."

Certainly, there is no magic power accorded to Bureaucrats which gives them power to perform physical wonders denied non-Bureaucrats. Generally, when this argument is set forth it is framed in a way which indicates that Government must do those things private enterprise cannot do. A more accurate interpretation might be that the Bureaucrats must do those things they want done which are physically possible, but which people will not voluntarily do themselves.

If the market situation is such that a new venture appears feasible, one individual (or many individuals banded together) will attempt to create the enterprise hoping to profit therefrom. Indeed, the entire history of private

entrepreneurship—as judged by the number of failures—
seems to indicate that businessmen are, if anything, over-
optimistic and frequently visualize opportunities which
later turn out to have been non-existent. Therefore, when
Bureaucrats speak of doing things private enterprise can't
do, they mean that individuals, after assessing the situation, are not willing to risk their own money in the under-
taking for fear of losing their funds or because better
opportunities exist elsewhere.

Bureaucrats, spending someone else's money, are not so
cautious. They may propose, and create, a new dam, rec-
reation area or faster flying commercial plane, without
worrying about what kind of return—if any—will be
realized from the investment.

3. *Government must provide essential services.*

As stated in number 2. People cannot provide what
people cannot provide; therefore this category is meant to
imply that government must provide important services at
less than market price or without cost to the user. Obviously, there is no such thing as *free* goods, as "manna"
falling from the sky, as it were; *free* schools, roads, and
the rest must be paid for by someone.

In providing these services at less than market price (or
free) to the user, the effects of setting prices too low invariably appear. There is a permanent scarcity. The government may increase schools and highways, parking areas
and public beaches, by 10% without satisfying the demand. It may increase them by 25%, 50%—or even

double them—and still not supply the demand. There is quite simply no limit to the demand for *free goods*.

If a private business firm sees an increased demand for its product the management is overjoyed and rushes to implement additional production. An increase in the demand for government services provided *free*, or at substantially less cost than market price, is regarded as a great problem.

    4. *It is all right for government to be in business, if it operates like a business.*

In addition to the absolute impossibility that Bureaucrats can operate a business as if it were a private enterprise (as discussed above) this statement contains its own implicit contradiction. For if private business is to be emulated and copied, and is, indeed, the standard for what is proper—why not have private business, altogether? There would then be no necessity for government in business.

Chapter 14

THE FOUR HORSEMEN OF THE NEW WORLD

Monopoly

We have been looking at the various ways in which Bureaucrats impinge upon *Consumers' Capitalism* in an attempt to manage the economy. We have discovered how direct curtailment, fiscal policy, restriction and encouragement, and price setting, cause repercussions in the economy far beyond their immediate points of application.

Now we shall examine what are considered the major economic "problems" of our age.

A great deal of attention has been paid to monopoly (or partial monopoly), and the problem of administered prices. Emotional Economics pictures a fat, greedy businessman in his easy chair, puffing a long cigar; while millions of poor people stand in line with the money to pay for his luxury-priced product.

In the real world of private industry, tough, fast-paced competition is the rule of the day, and companies are hard pressed to earn three or four pennies out of each sale's dollar. The difficulties of a private company obtaining a monopoly in a system of *Consumers' Capitalism* have already been discussed. There are monopolies, however, in any system of partial *Bureaucratic Capitalism*. The government may lend its power of coercion to private organizations, or may exert it directly; and monopoly evolves.

Some of the most basic parts of the economy are subject to administered prices—that is, prices fixed by bureaucratic dictate, rather than by the market. Prices for agricultural commodities, gold transportation, communications, energy, labor and money are administered in various degrees. And they are administered, not by private businessmen (for no individual or company is capable of making such prices stick), but by Bureaucrats.

The customer, in a system of *Consumers' Capitalism*, need not be subject to the price whims of an individual entrepreneur because he can take his business elsewhere if he so chooses. When the government sets the price for gold, cotton, hauling of freight, and other such commodities, the customer is helpless.

Unemployment

The evils of unemployment have been so thoroughly publicized, and the possible causes (such as poor schooling, poverty, slums, etc.) so minutely examined and documented, that to begin, we must step back and try to see the problem in a more comprehensive perspective.

Unemployment is an economic phenomenon, occurring in the production/consumption activities of man, and its causes must therefore be rooted in economics. People with something to sell cannot find buyers; workers, offering labor service on the market cannot find employers willing to purchase these services. Why?

In the previous discussions of theory there has been only one instance given wherein the market will not absorb all the factors offered for sale. That instance is when prices are too high.

In the unemployment phenomenon, we see an example of this economic law in operation. As long as wage rates are fixed at an artificially high level there will be unemployment; as long as there is unemployment, we know that wage rates are higher than the market will pay. This law is absolutely, universally true; and will remain so, regardless of how much legislation is passed, or what measures may be taken to relieve the unemployment situation.

Usually, wage rates are set at such artificially high levels by coercive monopoly, or partial monopoly. The government may raise wages by such devices as minimum wage laws, overtime provisions, setting standards for working conditions, taxing employers on payrolls, etc. Or, the government may lend its power—by either outright or subtle means—to labor unions, so they will be able to enforce higher wage demands for their members than the market has indicated. When a union member collects a higher wage rate through the power of the union he has gained privately, but it is a gain which must be paid for by someone else.

If the bricklayer gets a higher wage by union fiat there may be two immediate consequences. Construction of brick buildings will become more expensive, raising the price of housing so that all who use this housing must pay the resulting higher costs; or less brickwork will be done, and fewer bricklayers employed. Usually, both of these events occur at the same time; giving rise to the well-known fact that many unions with higher-than-average pay scales cannot find jobs for all their members and so must sharply limit new members, in addition to restraining others from engaging in their craft.

Denied access to higher paying jobs (due to the scarcity of such jobs and coercive union control over them), the remaining workers are displaced into areas where employment is not so tightly controlled; and the increased competition for jobs drives wages down in the freer areas.

In our example, the higher wages of the bricklayer are paid for by the lower wages of the other workers, and by the fact that fewer bricklayers are being employed. If an attempt should be made to enforce higher wages throughout the economy there will be a perpetual surplus of workers, as employers—forever held in check by consumer demand—are unable to employ workers at higher rates.

The term, "high rates," as it is used here, means high in the sense of relative market price, rather than any specific dollar and cents amount. The process of unemployment, caused by rates higher than the market price, occurs on different wage levels according to the state of the economy, the productivity of the workers, and the amount of coercion involved.

The legal minimum wage rate does not contribute to unemployment in the steel industry, since productivity and demand has already set the wages for steel workers far above the legal level. If there is unemployment in the steel industry it is because the supply-demand market price for steelworkers' services has been violated by something other than a minimum wage law. The legal minimum actually pushes all those who are less productive into unemployment.

In a productive economy with a minimum wage rate, such as in the United States, it is no accident that the increasing majority of the unemployed are young people, many of whom are persons with little work experience, less than average education, etc. *The minimum wage law has sentenced them to unemployment.*

To have full employment at wages higher than market rates is impossible; but the Bureaucrats seek an escape from this truism by various short-term measures. These measures are never effective over the long haul, so unemployment appears again and again, reminding us there are some things which legislative fiat cannot change.

One such measure is payments to the unemployed. Unfortunately, this does not alleviate unemployment, but only serves to make unemployment, as an issue, politically safe. The closer these payments approach wage levels, the more they tend to perpetuate unemployment.

Some economists have proposed inflation as a way of securing full employment. Their reasoning goes something like this:

"For reasons of politics it is felt that wage demands must be met. When they are thus pushed above the market rate, unemployment will result. An ensuing inflation will tend to raise all prices, but the prices of commodities and manufactured goods will rise faster and further than wage rates. This represents, in actuality, a comparative drop in wage rates vis-a-vis other prices and restores the wage rate more nearly to the market rate. Consequently, the restored ratio of wage rates to other prices will lessen unemployment."

Many things are wrong with this scheme. Even if we were to assume that inflation were harmless, few people are so economically naive as to be unable to notice a rise in prices; and if, from political necessity, wage demands must be met once, they must be met again and again. Modern day contracts and wage claims, based on increased living costs, have made this method obsolete—even for those insidious enough to recommend it.

The favorite ruse of the Bureaucrats for reducing unemployment is the creation of government make-work projects. Great tasks are undertaken; those out of work are given jobs; the new jobholders spend, creating more jobs; etc. An ideal solution, with one exception: it never works out that way!

The true outcome is entirely different, with the final conclusion dependent upon which method the government chooses to pay the people employed in its make-work projects. If it pays them by printing the money for their pay envelopes, inflation is created. If the government pays out of taxation, it merely transfers the direction of the economy from the taxpayers to the Bureaucrats. The taxpayers can buy less, and support fewer factories and workers than before; while the Bureaucrats (with taxpayers' money) can support more workers than before. New jobs are created by the government, but not as rapidly as the old ones are simultaneously being destroyed through increased taxation.

From a practical point of view, a war is the best make-work project ever devised. With a war to be won it is never a problem to obtain funds for proposed supplies or construction; during peacetime the building of additional bridges, roads, etc., might cause argument. With a war, taxes can be increased with little resistance from taxpayers; prime workers are taken out of the labor market and into the army; and a great lift is given the economy as potential shortages are envisioned in the future.

Except for brief periods of war, America has had institutional unemployment for so long that it is difficult for many workers to imagine a situation where it would not exist. Thousands of new laws and billions of dollars in subsidies have not succeeded in making enough jobs. In a nation where there are more people who want to work than there are jobs available, not only the unemployed, but also the employed, are being ill-served.

A spectre hangs over those who work, for to lose one's job can become a real hardship. The workers inside are separated from the unemployment lines outside only by the ability to hold onto their jobs. Younger men are made the enemies of the older because youth may be regarded as a premium, with those who possess it being given job preference; union members, lest they be displaced, seek to limit admittance of newcomers; white men are afraid of being pushed out by minorities. People are thus divided into antagonistic groups as they seek to protect their jobs.

On the other hand, in *Consumers' Capitalism* there is a built-in system of unemployment insurance. If a man leaves his job he can find another employer, or may go into business for himself. Under the conditions imposed by a free market he must accommodate himself to the wishes of the consumer in order to secure the best paying job available—working in those lines of endeavor and at the pay-scale the consumer (as an aggregate force) has determined. But in so doing, he would have a freedom unknown to many men in a hampered market. He could work if he wanted to.

Depression

One of the most nagging questions in the study of economics has been the problem of general business fluctuations. Again and again, the pendulum of economic activity has swung from periods of prosperity and well-being, to periods of depression and unnecessary hardship. Modern economies have followed this pattern for so long that economists have even tried to trace an exact time element in the fluctuations, in the hope of being able to predict when the next stage of the cycle is due.

So far, these efforts have been unsuccessful. All we can know for sure is that fluctuations do occur from time to time—some mild, some severe; and that they are of a Boom/Bust character—or, to be more precise, a never-varying round of Inflation-Crisis-Recession-Depression-Recovery/Inflation-Crises . . . and so on.

When we speak of business fluctuations, we mean the average economy in general. Individual businesses or industries can and do have cycles of their own, caused by any number of specific factors. The construction industry may vary from month to month because of weather conditions; the men's belt industry may undergo a private depression when men convert to beltless pants; the cigar industry may be in a long-term downtrend which may be reversed by a cigarette cancer scare; etc.

In a free market adjustments are continually being made to such changing conditions as the market takes new data into consideration in its march toward equilibrium. Personal shiftings of fortune occur normally; the regulating mechanism of *Consumers' Capitalism* is such that any mistakes an individual makes are borne chiefly by that individual, and will not drag the entire economy down with him.

During a general business depression there may be some businesses which run counter to the trend and prosper, but the majority of enterprises suffer. Sales fall off. Goods made and sold so readily just yesterday or a few months ago will no longer move at the previous volume for the same prices.

There is a sudden revelation of massive mistakes on all levels of the economy, with the greatest errors usually occurring in the capital goods industries. Profits vanish; bankruptcies and foreclosures increase. Uncertainty and pessimism take over, as firms—so recently going full blast —try to cut back, in order to survive. Unemployment climbs while production falls, and investments decline in value. "Hard times" come upon the nation.

To explain why this happens, a multitude of theories has been propounded including that of the anarchy of production, insufficient investment media, uneven investment, too much investment, too much saving, shortage of money, hoarding, underconsumption, overconsumption, consumption by the wrong people, overproduction, uneven production, coincidence of individual cycles, labor-saving machinery, waves of innovation, wages of replacement, difficulties in forecasting, rate of population growth, migrations, war, peace, public opinion, magnetic absorptions and sun spots.

Some of these theories are quite far-fetched, even when couched in official-sounding language and dressed up in mathematical mumbo-jumbo. Others contain some grain of truth which, upon closer examination, reveals itself as merely descriptive of a particular symptom; hence, not a real explanation of the depression at all.

Perhaps the whole aura of fear surrounding the subject of depressions and cycles stems from the fact that so many contradictory ideas have been put forward to explain them, and that most such explanations are insufficient. Economic theory has taken a number of wrong turns, into dead-end streets. At the inception of economics as a disciplined body of thought, inaccurate theories of depression were understandable, since it was not possible to dissect and understand cycles until a meaningful subjective theory of value had been developed.

Despite this advance in thinking, a great many economists still continued to attack the problem by starting with the basic assumption that such cycles are an inherent, built-in feature of the market system. Either through habit, or because they prefer it this way, they continue to turn out variations on the same old theme.

However, other men, in seeing that a long list of insufficient theories stemmed from this premise, began to reason from the other direction—that cycles are not an integral part of the market system—and a full and consistent theory of depressions has been developed.

Economic activity is connected and interrelated. Bust follows Boom, and is a reaction to the Boom. Depression is dependent upon the preceding Boom in order to evolve just as the recovery stage after the depression is dependent upon the preceding depression. (Cause and effect/cause and effect.)

Since we have discarded the preceding hypothesis (that this cycle is the basic pattern of a free market), it follows we must look for some outside interference which can hinder the market's drive toward equilibrium. A seed is planted, foreign to the free market but nonetheless affecting it, and grows into bitter fruit. If we will now turn to an examination of the Inflation/Boom period we shall see where depressions start, why they come into being, and who makes them.

Inflation

In searching for a cause of business fluctuations we have reached a point where we are now looking for an outside interference, impinging upon the market system. An unhampered free market has an irrepressible tendency to build itself into an ever-better position in order to provide maximum consumer satisfaction (within the limits of whatever resources are available to it).

Individual members of the economy are responsible for this tendency, usually unaware that due to division of labor and lack of compulsion they are hooked into a system which ties their own economic success to increasing the material benefits of everyone else. If the "producer" (which can be taken to mean every working man and woman) wants to prosper, he must produce more of what the consumer wants. There is no other way. Planning for this kind of market is done individually, by the most capable entrepreneurs, laboring within their own specialties and applying their knowledge, experience, and understanding to the pertinent information.

In this manner the economic process continues to be refined and improved; growing in a logical pattern which is consistent with the actual state of affairs as it is reflected daily in the market place. True, some entrepreneurs may err in their judgment and make mistakes, consequently being eliminated from their planning level; but to the extent which men are rational in business matters, mistakes will not happen on a scale large enough to disrupt all production/consumption activity.

What would happen, however, if personal, private, individual economic action no longer coincided with the efficient functioning of the general economy? Obviously, the system would break down. The super-efficient, vastly complicated specializations existing under the division of labor could not continue as efficaciously as before, because individuals would no longer have a true guide to show them how to specialize. Men cannot make shoes profitably unless there are other men willing and able to buy them.

The breakdown comes about through distortions in the

normal market process which mask the economic reality based on consumer wants. These distortions are caused by inflation. A free economy builds itself, gradually, into a state of maximum material satisfaction for its members because individual producers act according to signals from the consumer. By distorting and confusing these market signals, inflation aborts the movement toward equilibrium, thereby causing a breakdown.

Inflation, in popular terminology, has come to mean a general increase in prices throughout the economy. Originally, the economic definition of inflation was, "an increase in the money supply, not backed by specie".

Though both definitions are similar, and an increase in money supply eventually will lead to rising prices, it is necessary, for the sake of clarity, to draw a distinction between these two definitions, and to use the latter when we talk about inflation.

A general price rise is difficult to chart over the short term (there is a good deal of question as to the accuracy of "cost of living" indexes), and can often be seen clearly only in retrospect. Also, some of the additional increased money may leave the country for a time and be hoarded abroad, thus temporarily mitigating its price-raising effects at home.

The most important point, when we speak of a rise in prices, is that we mean prices are higher than they would have been without inflation. All other things being equal, increased production will lower prices; if greater output is concurrent with increase in money supply, dollar and cents prices may not change very much. Instead of dropping they stay the same. Hence, a reliance based solely upon rising prices as an indication of inflation may be misleading, particularly during the early stages.

To see how inflation distortion works, let us take an example. Suppose a group of men get together and set up a shop capable of turning out perfect counterfeit money. Each day they run off a batch and distribute it to the members of the gang; each day these men go to the stores, their pockets bulging, and buy whatver they want. They do not add to the productive stream in any way, yet have increased their demand for economic goods and services.

Meanwhile, producers in the market are busily calculating on the basis of dollars and cents, as always. Each entrepreneur throughout the country is observing what is happening in his special field, and adjusting his production to the signals the market gives. He is unaware that in a distant city a group of men are printing counterfeit money.

The more money these counterfeiters print, the more is put into circulation. Imperceptibly at first, then in growing degrees, their spending of the new artificial dollars begins to make itself felt in the market as demand for economic goods; causing shifts in productive activities in order to take the new demand into account.

As a result, the real producers in the economy get fewer

goods than they would have otherwise, since they are now sharing the total output with the counterfeiters.

The counterfeit money represents an addition to the money supply; more dollars now are bid for the same amount of goods as before; and prices rise. All prices do not go up at the same time, or by the same proportions; some prices rise here, some there—further distorting the picture. Due to the higher prices, the counterfeiters find themselves on a treadmill; if they want to maintain their standard of living they must put out even larger amounts of money.

Eventually, one of two things may happen. The counterfeiters may print so much money that prices will begin to rise at a noticeably accelerated pace. Everyone will become aware of the inflation, and people will pay little attention to money, realizing it is becoming worthless. When this occurs, existing money begins to lose its value altogether.

Let us say, however, that our counterfeiters possess a modicum of foresight and wish to avoid a runaway inflation, with its attendant aftermath of hardship and potential social upheaval. Before the inflation reaches the crack-up stage they decide to stop, or to slow up considerably, their printing of counterfeit money.

When they do, something happens which they have not counted on. The economy has been geared to taking the counterfeiters' demand as genuine; working itself into a structure which assumed this demand to be a part of the actual economy. Suddenly, this demand (based upon counterfeit money) is gone—but the factories, machines, trained workers, channels of distribution, production processes and interrelated economic activities, inaugurated in response to the counterfeiters' demand, is still in existence and functioning. Certainly it cannot continue to function in the same manner as before.

A violent change occurs. Because of the differing proportion of demand between the counterfeiters and everyone else, business must now be reorganized in order to coincide with the new state of affairs.

This reorganization is called *depression*.

Our example is an elementary one, with many oversimplifications. No gang of counterfeiters is capable of turning out so much money without being caught; we have merely used the comparison to illustrate how an increase in the money supply can have a distortive effect on the economy. With such an example as background, we can proceed to see what happens in an actual situation.

So long as individuals used gold for money there was no way to tamper with the money supply; only a new discovery of a tremendously large vein of gold could drastically increase the amount in circulation. When gold was done away with as a medium of exchange, put under government control, and its place taken by a paper standard, the Bureaucrats were given the power to turn out additional money.

In discussing government finance and price-fixing we

have described how Bureaucrats may make new money by creating additional bank deposits—which is the equivalent of cranking up the printing presses. It becomes apparent that when the government manufactures more money, it creates inflation.

The government may create additional money from what appears to be the best of all possible motives—to help the people—but consequences of an act are never changed because of good intentions. When it comes to economic effect, inflationary policies put the Bureaucrats in exactly the same position, vis-a-vis the economy, as the counterfeiters of our illustration.

When new paper money (or credit) is created, the creators, and their favorites, get a free ride. They have a dollar they didn't have before; moreover, it is a dollar they have not earned by engaging in productive work. Yet, when they go into the marketplace with their new money, a dollar is a dollar is a dollar—it mingles and spends the same as all other dollars.

There is no corresponding increase in real wealth, to match the new money. The same amount of goods are available as before, and with more money being bid for these goods, prices are pushed to a higher level than they would have reached under normal circumstances.

The process is much like watering the soup. Someone adds a cup of water to the pot, stirs it, and takes out a cup of the new mixture. He added water and took out broth; there are still as many cups of broth remaining in the pot; only now, each serving will be slightly diluted, and contain a little less sustenance. One of the tragedies of inflation is that unless one has a sensitive palate he might not notice a difference in his share of the pot until a goodly amount of watering has been done. In this manner inflation becomes a silent, hidden tax on all who contribute to the production process.

One of mankind's fondest dreams is a low interest rate, and plentiful money. Through control of the monetary and banking systems, government officials have the apparent ability to fulfill this ever-popular desire. They merely turn out more money.

Let us follow the process which takes place when the Bureaucrats embark on a policy of cheap and easy money. First, they move to allow expansion of bank deposit money. The resulting influx of new money enters the loan market on the supply side, and lowers the interest rates. Money is now both cheaper and more plentiful. The government has taken the route of credit expansion to inflate the currency.

Before further examination of this inflationary process, it is necessary to review the crucial role played by interest within *Consumer's Capitalism*. The rate of interest in a free market, expresses the relationship between the public desire for short-term economic satisfaction and long-term satisfaction. The savings of individuals (meaning their foregone consumption) allows the collection of monies which represents later want-satisfaction, rather than immediate want-satisfaction.

We must be careful to characterize money saved through foregone consumption as a kind of real wealth, and in this sense view it as a store of value—a ticket to be exchanged for real wealth, which the individual has earned but has chosen not yet to cash in. He loans his ticket to someone else, who does redeem it—in the form of capital goods. These goods are available precisely because the funds being used for purchase represent real wealth, which the lender has not yet used.

Money, seen in this perspective, is consistent with economic reality. When additional money is created by printing new paper, or making penned entries in bank ledgers (with no corresponding creation of real wealth), the money is artificial; it is money by fiat.

We have noted in a previous section how the entrepreneur bids for this available fund of savings, and through this action sets the interest rate. His bidding is determined by the profitability of his business, since the most profitable enterprise is best able to borrow. Hence, the interest rate, as with all prices in *Consumer's Capitalism*, becomes a way of rationing the available supply.

The most capable borrower—as judged by his consumer acceptance—has access to the economy's reservoir of savings, and in this manner diverts these savings into capital accumulation which is approved by the consumer.

During a credit expansion the fiat money becomes available on the loan market where making loans becomes easier, with interest costs below normal. The entrepreneur moves to adjust to the new conditions, which would seemingly indicate the availability of more capital for use in increased production.

Actual real wealth available for conversion into capital goods is no more plentiful than before. What has become more plentiful is fiat money—paper and bank credit— and as the entrepreneur borrows the new money the rationing system will no longer be as stringent. Capital investments (of which the consumer does not really approve) will be initiated, for which there is no corresponding real savings. When these investments are transformed into stone and steel the factors of such production are necessarily prevented from usage in other areas which would have had more approval.

At first, the credit expansion gives an illusion that miracles are being worked. There appears to be more life in the marketplace as the new money acts as a quick charge to boost business. Then, although it is not at once apparent, prices begin the inevitable, gradual rise.

The individual closest to the new money comes out best—at least, temporarily. His purchasing power is increased before there is an increase in his costs, giving him a gain at the expense of someone else farther down the line. Costs and selling prices are distorted by the influx of money.

As the Boom continues, people are aware of the upward price spiral but for the present a great many seem to be doing well. Wages continue to rise as employers bid for workers' services; and employees, with their additional wages, add to the demand for goods so that producers see gains in sales despite higher prices. Business firms compile handsome profit statements, not realizing that inflation has caused traditional accounting procedure to mis-state the real picture. Equipment and inventory (valued at cost) do not reflect the inflation which has taken place since their acquisition, so profits are overstated. Real estate and stock prices rise, with the advance considered to be a gain in the real wealth rather than an increase in value which matches the higher cost of living.

Feeling prosperous, some people spend their apparent gains; in actuality, they are spending their capital. Producers who did not seek to borrow the easy money for expanded production when it first became available are now forced to borrow, because continuing production at the former level is costing more money.

Everywhere, there is activity. All markets are booming, business is bustling, workers are sought-after, prices are going up and up. Confidence feeds upon itself, adding a spirit of optimism and expectations of eternally bright tomorrows.

Such a utopia cannot last forever. So unrealistic a foundation as the government printing office or the bureaucratic direction of banks is not enough to inaugurate a period of prosperity. To keep the Boom going, one shot of new money is insufficient; for once it is loaned out

the market rate of interest will reassert itself and the
Boom will taper off. New money must be constantly fed
into the loan market to keep the Boom going.

Lest the situation escalate into runaway inflation where
money becomes worthless the authorities or banks must,
at some point, begin cutting back new money formation.
This particular measure may be undertaken at various
levels, so that the credit expansion Boom/Inflation described here may range from a development which is
barely perceptible to serious dislocation of a great part of
the economy.

When the entry of new money on the market ceases,
the easy money starts to disappear. The interest rate tends
to rise; loans which once were granted so freely are
no longer granted. Business cannot continue to obtain
cheap money for its operations; and production, based
upon the illusion of such money, becomes unprofitable
now that the money is not available. With the inflationary
pressures lessened or removed the consumer reasserts his
decision-making power over the economy, and the consequent shift in demand leaves many items unable to fetch
selling prics high enough to cover inflated production costs.

Maladjustments are now uncovered throughout the
economy, particularly in the capital goods industries;
where investments which seemed so promising under the
artificial state of affairs are seen—by the harsh light of
economic realism—to be duds. Scarce real capital has been
invested in the wrong areas. Production facilities have

been created and workers trained to turn out products for which there is insufficient demand; while the consumer wishes to buy other goods which are not being produced in sufficient amounts. There has been neither overinvestment nor underconsumption, but rather, incorrect investment.

The reorientation of production/consumption activity —the depression—now takes place. Business begins to adjust to the new market conditions and, in accordance with the extent of exaggeration of the preceding Boom, realignment must be accomplished as the market seeks to move toward equilibrium. If the Boom was mild, adjustment may be mild: a recession. If the Boom was big, the correction must necessarily correspond.

The end of the Boom may ease into a recession or be turned into a panic by some minor event—even a chance happening. Some entrepreneurs, unable to obtain easy money, are forced to dump their goods on the market for whatever they will bring, and prices suddenly drop. More and more people, recognizing the impending depression, become frightened. Firms need loans to stay afloat, and the economic outlook is such that few want to lend.

The counter-effect of the Boom now takes place. Sales fall off, businesses go bankrupt, factories close, workers are laid off. Optimism and confidence, which had once reigned supreme, turns to pessimism and despair.

The depression stage makes the recovery stage possible. It is during this period that the bad investments come to light, and are abandoned or written down to their real value as gauged by the demands of the consumer. Wasteful and inefficient enterprises fall by the wayside. Costs, including labor, descend to a level where they can be absorbed by the consumer in making his purchases.

During this reorganization the resulting shift in the economy does not take place smoothly. It is agitated by frictions developed during the preceding inflationary periods, and by the fact that it takes a certain amount of time for realignments to be made. Many people will be hurt financially as the market goes through the rough upheaval and painful readjustment necessary before it can move once again toward a balance.

Each Boom/Bust cycle, in every time and place, has a history uniquely its own. There are similarities between them, but varying conditions and individual circumstances will show up in different ways.

Economics is forever describing a current situation which is undergoing continual change. Contrasting effects may change some of the familiar Boom/Bust guideposts. Some prices may not rise during the inflation, or credit expansion may not cause an immediate Boom. If the entrepreneur expects the government to tax away his profits, or if he makes a dismal estimate of the future state of the market, he has insufficient incentive for borrowing. (There is evidence that such was the case during the New Deal; and is one of the theories put forth to explain the failure of massive "pump-priming" which was to have started a Boom recovery from the Great Depression).

Men have had a great deal of telling experiences with credit expansion Booms of the sort outlined in this chapter, and it may be they have become more aware of the distortive effect of easy money, and less susceptible to it. On the other hand, the more recent development of inflation via government deficits will result in no fewer distortions.

Bureaucratic interference in the marketplace, through heavy tax burdens and innumerable rules and regulations, personifies the distortive effects of inflation and magnifies the hardship during subsequent reorganization. Any governmental tampering makes the market less flexible and less adaptable to changing conditions, rendering it less able to fulfill its functions. On the upswing of a credit expansion, investments are encouraged into favorite areas, making costs higher. During the ensuing depression, prices, wages, and interest are prevented from seeking equilibrium, and the market does not clear. All who want to buy cannot buy, and those wanting to sell cannot sell. Whatever prices are held artificially high, the net effect is that the unfortunates last in line cannot find a market for their goods or services.

In this way, the textbook signs of cyclical movements, which are sharp fluctuations in prices and wages (and consequently, sharp fluctuations in individual income), have come to be softened. Distortions show up, instead, as fluctuations in production and employment. In place of a general drop in wages, modern mild recessions tend to follow a pattern in which workers who are able to keep their jobs do about as well as before. The brunt is borne by those who cannot find employment.

If production and employment are off it is argued that a credit expansion will alleviate the condition. An injection of new money will supposedly call all the idle workers, unused factories, farms, mines, etc., back into productive use. We have already discussed the futility of printing paper and calling it real wealth.

The argument for credit expansion fails to take into consideration the fact that large amounts of unused factors of production are not an adjunct to *Consumers' Capitalism*. Unused factors are leftovers from previous cycles which have not yet adjusted to the real state of the market as judged by consumer preferences.

In order for such factors to become employed, their asking price must be brought down to meet the going price on the market. If, through inflation, money-prices are instead raised to meet the asking price of these factors, it may seem that the market has been responsible; whereas, in actuality, only the money-prices have risen and we are again confronted with economic distortion. Real prices (after allowing for inflation) will still bear some relationship to the situation as it existed before the inflation.

Earlier, we discussed how the preceding argument has been put forward in order to fool working people into accepting lower real wages while they are supposedly being deceived by higher dollar rates. As another example, Mr. Baker owns an unused factory which he wishes to rent at $1,000 per month. He is unable to rent it at that price, but will not lower the rent. An inflation begins, and five years later he is able to rent the plant at the desired price. If he thinks he has accomplished his objectives he is kidding himself; for the $1,000 is worth less now than it was five years earlier when he set the price, due to inflation. He has confused money with purchasing power.

Briefly, the cause of these business fluctuations is this:

The ever-present drive of a free market toward maximum consumer satisfaction is warped by interference. Unhindered, the entire economy would not find itself without investment capital next year because it was force-fed this year, or because it expanded too much capital in the wrong places.

When the government intervenes (as it does in the case of inflation), economic reality becomes distorted by a shimmering, illusory money-mask. Men are unknowingly deceived. The partnership whereby profitable individual economic activity benefits the economy as a whole is dissolved. Personal efforts to enrich oneself cease to be identifiable with actions which enrich others. Eventually, when the movement has gone far astray and enough errors have accumulated, reorganization becomes necessary.

During the Boom, mistakes are made on a wholesale

basis because individuals can't see what is happening. A depression is the unveiling of these mistakes; the correction of them is the recovery.

Part V

BEFORE AND BEYOND
ECONOMICS

Chapter 15

VALUE CHOICES

Underlying Assumptions

Economics describes one aspect of human behavior. We began this study by reviewing how an individual (Robinson Crusoe) acts within the sphere of economics; and from there we traced production/consumption activities of millions of people living in a complex society.

To be accurate we must be sure to limit economic inquiry to its exact function, which is describing social relationships on the production/consumption level. We have tried to put aside bias while we examined the facts and followed the argument wherever it led.

In explaining Crusoe's actions it was necessary to make one implicit assumption (in order that we might concentrate on economics without becoming involved in other areas of study).

We assumed that Crusoe had the right to do whatever he wished in the economic realm. He could pick his own values. This freedom did not mean he could trancend all physical limitations (whether his own, or those of the island), since no man can completely do that.

However, in arranging those matters over which he could exert control he was able to do whatever pleased him. He could harvest coconuts, fish, or swim; and there was no one to restrain him by force from doing those things. Within such circumstances we defined the choices he made as free; they were obviously the choices he expected to be most gratifying.

At the next step in our economic survey, we found it necessary to re-focus our picture from the viewing of one individual, to a scope which included all of society. Where there are many men, rather than one, and activity is interrelated, individual free choice within the realm of economics is no longer so easily defined.

The term, "free choice" still indicates the right of the individual to select production/consumption activity which he believes will best please him (within his physical and environmental limitations). But when more than one person is involved, free choice, by its very nature, must be expanded to include everyone.

Such expansion necessitates a just system of property rights; and the property rights of others subsequently become part of the individual's environmental limitations.

Economics—either by itself, or through its logical deductions—can neither establish, nor validate, a social order built upon property rights. The rightness or wrongness of free choice in matters economic, and the property rights which make this free choice possible, must be decided by philosophy.

We have assumed, in this exposition of economics, that Crusoe was entitled to free choice; and on the basis of this assumption we proceed to explain his behavior. Consistently, the same assumption was made with which to examine economic activity of people living in a complex society.

Using an assumption of free choice as the standard, we have found that *Consumers' Capitalism* will be more nearly satisfactory than any other; for under its formulas production of the most-wanted items will be maximized; while, at the same time, men are enjoying the greatest possible freedom. Seen from this standard, a complete system of *Bureaucratic Capitalism* is both absurd, and unworkable.

Another Point Of View

Portions of *Bureaucratic Capitalism* may be super-imposed upon a free market system (as in a *Mixed Economy*), and the inhabitants suffer in direct proportion to the amount of bureaucratic control applied. We can observe this theory in action in the contemporary world by surveying those nations having the greatest degree of bureaucratic national planning (as in China, India, Russia, Cuba and so on). These are the nations which comparatively have the severest shortages of economic goods, and where the populace lives on the lower levels of material prosperity.

In the freer countries of the west, shortages are confined to those areas (such as schools, roads, parking, postal service, etc.) over which the Bureaucrats exercise the most control.

When a government exceeds its basic function (which is that of protecting its citizens from domestic and foreign criminals), and begins to mix Economics with Politics, the citizenry is divided into several groups which must eventually conflict. Governmental intervention creates a group of net taxpayers, and a group of net tax receivers; those who have jobs, and those who do not; those granted monopoly privileges, and those who must deal with the monopolies; those who have high fixed prices and others who have low fixed prices; those who will be hurt by legislation, and others who will be benefited; and so on.

In every case, one group gains at the expense of another, and the makers of law become powerful men, capable of determining individual economic fate.

In such circumstances we may observe a hardening of the status quo as people try to protect their positions by legislation; while lobbies and pressure tactics are used by organizations as a means to gain the Bureaucrats' benign influence. In those places where a civil rights/economic rights dichotomy exists, groups parade and demonstrate to gain government favors. Witnessing this spectacle, officials with a flair for public relations have suggested that the consumer ought to have a lobby of his own, to protect his interests.

This idea, while inspirational, misses the point—for there is no interventionary legislation which can possibly benefit the consumer as a whole. His aggregate interest lies in assuring greater production of those things which are considered most worthwhile—a process which can be reached only through measures of less restriction, not more.

For the consumer, every economic law passed means waste, and lessened consumption opportunities. The Bureaucrats, with their laws and tampering, create an unreal economic world from the consumer's point of view.

In this unreal world, economic activity does not correspond with the totality of consumer demand; yet the consumer, unaware of the bureaucratically-created distortion, continues to act upon his own value choices. When the distance between the reality of consumer desires and distorted economic activity becomes large enough, a breakdown will occur.

In a free state of *Consumers' Capitalism* such a breakdown would not be possible because this conflict of values between Bureaucrats and consumers would not exist. No man could direct another's choice.

The First and Last Question

In the final analysis, we find that economics is simple after all. It is simple because at rock-bottom any economic system is a means for achieving certain ends, rather than an end in itself.

We have described various forms the production/consumption mechanism may take, and have shown that the answer to the question of which may be the best form to use does not rest within the structures themselves. Rather, this conclusion is dependent upon the goals which are sought.

It is possible to understand economics as a system of social exchange, answering the basic material questions. It is not possible, in good faith, to conscientiously express preference for any particular variant, unless one has answered the most fundamental question of all:

"What ends, goals, and objectives do I want an economic system to attain?"